In Common Cause

Books by John W. Gardner

IN COMMON CAUSE

THE RECOVERY OF CONFIDENCE

NO EASY VICTORIES

SELF-RENEWAL

EXCELLENCE

JOHN W. GARDNER

In Common Cause

W · W · NORTON & COMPANY · INC ·
NEW YORK

Library of Congress Cataloging in Publication Data

Gardner, John William, 1912–
  In common cause.

  1. Common Cause (U. S.) 2. Political
participation—United States. I. Title.
JK1118.G36   322.4'3'0973   72–6136
ISBN 0–393–06338–0

Published simultaneously in Canada
by George J. McLeod Limited, Toronto
PRINTED IN THE UNITED STATES OF AMERICA

  2 3 4 5 6 7 8 9 0

Dedicated to the Members of Common Cause

Contents

ACKNOWLEDGMENTS		11
INTRODUCTION		15
CHAPTER ONE	Politics and Government	23
CHAPTER TWO	The Game of Barter and Purchase	33
CHAPTER THREE	Access	44
CHAPTER FOUR	Responsiveness and Accountability	59
CHAPTER FIVE	Citizen Action	72
CHAPTER SIX	Effectiveness in Citizen Action	85
CHAPTER SEVEN	First Steps in a Long Journey	97
APPENDIX A	The First Year of Common Cause	112
APPENDIX B	Governing Board of Common Cause	124
APPENDIX C	Members' Ratings of Issues	127

Acknowledgments

A<small>S</small> USUAL, my debts are many.

First of all, my thanks to those who commented on the manuscript or helped in other ways with the books—David Cohen, Thomas Mathews, Robert Gallamore, Elizabeth Drew, Helen Rowan, Sally Roper, Joan Thompson, Helen Kaufman.

Second, my profound personal gratitude to those who have built Common Cause: those who created it—Lowell Beck, Thomas Mathews, Robert Meier, Georgianna Rathbun, John Lagomarcino, Roger Craver, Robert Gallamore, Richard Clark, Wendy Burdsall, Barbara Collins, Mary Hanson, John Wood, and others; those who brought it to maturity—Jack Conway, David Cohen, Craig Barnes, David Mixner, Robert Colodzin, Ken Smith, Carole Cohen, Ruth Saxe, Fred Wertheimer, David Dawson, Don Ainsworth, Pat Sabin, Lawrence Gilson, Mitchell Dorson, and others in a list too long to recite; and those incredibly faithful and gifted volunteers, of whom I cannot possibly acknowledge more than a few by name—people such as Lee and George Dolgin, Michael Walsh, Susan Herter, Harold Harris, Cynthia Lefferts, David Wilken, and many, many others.

To all of them: "This is your book."

In Common Cause

Introduction

IN SEPTEMBER 1970 a citizens' movement called Common Cause came into being. From the day of its birth it has exhibited extraordinary vitality. But it doesn't fit any of the familiar political categories; and this has led to bewilderment on the part of those who live by conventional categories.

There is little cause for bewilderment. Common Cause is pursuing an old American tradition: hard-hitting pressure on politicians to bring about results desired by citizens. It is better organized than most citizens' groups have been; and it is using techniques of professional organizing and lobbying that the citizen has rarely used in the past. But its basic activity is a familiar one. In America, when citizens have a concern they speak out. The members of Common Cause are speaking out— loud and clear.

Every informed American has heard the word "crisis" so often that he's bored by it. But under the boredom, he's troubled. No one needs to tell him about the problems. He breathes the dirty air. His children attend the crowded schools. He pays the cost of inflation and feels the economic squeeze. He suffers the consequences of the housing shortage. He bears the brunt of the breakdown in law enforcement and the administration of justice.

POLITICS AND GOVERNMENT

If we are to solve these problems, if we are ever to regain command of our situation, we must look first to our political and governmental institutions, for politics and government are the instruments through which we achieve our shared purposes, if we achieve them at all. No other nation in the world has enabled more citizens to fulfill their individual purposes, even their whims, than the United States. But we're not doing at all well with the purposes we all share and must pursue together—creating excellent public schools, protecting the environment, preserving livable communities, enforcing the law, administering justice.

We can move toward the solution of some of our problems through private-sector action. But sooner or later, in pursuing our shared purposes, we must turn to government and the political process. That's what government and politics are for. We can't lean on government, but in the accomplishment of our shared purposes we can't do without it. And the sad truth is that today our political and governmental apparatus is rickety and inadequate.

Even those Americans who are most interested in politics and government have tended to accept the limitations of the system as it now exists. They seem resigned to the fact that most state governments are incompetent, that most state legislatures are tragically inadequate, that most city government is so designed as to make governing impossible, that the Congress of the United States needs a thorough overhaul, that the political parties are too often unresponsive to the concerns of their own members, and that corruption runs rampant throughout the system.

The truth is that our political and governmental arrangements are so badly designed for contemporary purposes that they waste taxpayers' money and mismanage good programs. The citizen does not have access to them. They are not instruments of the popular will. They cannot be held accountable.

Effectiveness, access, responsiveness, accountability—these are the attributes we have a right to expect of our instruments of self-government. They do not characterize government today. Under present conditions, our political and governmental machinery cannot serve *anybody*—neither poor people nor the middle class, neither black nor white, neither young nor old. Even very gifted leaders can't make the machinery work.

It is not a question of efficiency for efficiency's sake. Government and politics will never be genuinely efficient; but when they are no longer responsive, when they can no longer be held accountable, then we all suffer. We spend billions of dollars to solve our problems and fail to solve them. We support a vast and intricate public machinery that does not in fact serve human needs. The consequences in unsolved public problems are familiar to everyone. Our society today is a society that has almost lost the capacity to manage itself.

The informed American is just beginning to grasp the seriousness of our situation. In the past, he has accepted the inadequacies of the public process as among the inevitable minor annoyances of life, like rainy days and head colds. But a good many citizens have worked with great energy and little success on the substantive problems of education, health, poverty, housing, employment, equal rights, the environment, and war and peace. And it is gradually beginning to dawn on them that many of those problems are made harder to solve

17

—or rendered wholly unsolvable—by breakdowns in the structure and process of government. They are beginning to see that the very instruments we must use to solve the nation's problems—the instruments of self-government—are themselves in need of repair. In short, our ailment is not a minor annoyance, such as a head cold, but more nearly comparable to a disease of the central nervous system, dangerously disabling and possibly terminal.

CITIZENS CAN ACT

Citizens can do something about the problems that plague this society. Common Cause has fought pitched battles on issues of the deepest concern to the American people—the Vietnam war, environmental pollution, racial injustice, poverty, unemployment, and women's rights. But this is not a book about those issues. It is about *what citizens must do in order to have a voice on those (or any other) issues.* In matters of social action, citizens have some lessons to learn. If they can't or won't learn, they condemn themselves to righteous impotence.

The first lesson they must learn is to repair the breakdown in the public process. They can demand access to their instruments of self-government. They can demand that public officials be responsive and accountable. They can advocate the public interest with the same persuasiveness that others advocate special interests. They can monitor the actions of both legislative and executive branches with the same high professional competence that the special interests bring to that task. They can go far toward eliminating the corrupting influence of money and secrecy in our public life.

Let's be specific. We don't need to let the boys in the back room control the nomination of candidates. We can open the doors and let the fresh air and the people in. We can open up the nominating process and make it honest.

We can develop a far better system of campaign financing than we now have. We can end the system in which too many of our "public servants" work out their terms in servitude to big donors.

We can require lobbying controls. We can insist upon full disclosure of conflict of interest on the part of every public official. We can demand "open meetings" legislation requiring that the public business be done publicly.

Such issues are rarely discussed by candidates—and that is no accident. These issues cut close to the bone. They are at the very heart of a system by which insiders preserve their power and prerogatives and exclude the ordinary citizen from access to decisions. They are at the heart of the breakdown of accountability in government.

Citizens can repair that breakdown—but only through organization. Common Cause has proven that it can be done. We have won enough battles, from the constitutional amendment for the eighteen-year-old voter to the campaign-spending legislation of 1972, to know the power of citizen action.

CONTINUOUS ACCOUNTABILITY

Common Cause intends to reestablish the link of accountability between the citizen and his elected representatives.

Today good citizens leave the voting booth, pat themselves on the back for doing their civic duty, and then go home and forget the whole thing. But the political machines don't forget it. The oil lobby doesn't forget it. Nor the agribusiness lobby. Representatives of those and all the other special interests are in their offices the morning after election day figuring out the next step. Cynics say that campaign promises are made to be broken, but the special-interest lobbyists don't depend on such promises. They have discovered the various ways of calling elected officials to account after the election. The citizen is going to have to take a leaf from their book.

Common Cause, by linking the long tradition of citizen action with the skills of professional lobbying is introducing a new ingredient into the political system, a means of assuring continuous accountability to the citizen—a means of voting between elections. We think it's time to give this nation back to its people. The basic ailments that are making invalids of our political and governmental institutions will only be cured by tough, sustained pressure. And that pressure must come from citizens.

THE BALLOT ISN'T ENOUGH

It is vitally important that we nominate the best possible candidates and then choose wisely from among them. But that isn't enough. Among a portion of our citizens—a steadily diminishing portion—there survives the wistful hope that if we just elect the right person we will all be saved. But the cool voice of experience says something different. It reminds us that regardless of who wins, the death grip of the seniority system will still paralyze Congress. The revenue and appropriations committees will still operate like secret societies. The Finance Committee of the Senate and the Ways and

Means Committee of the House will continue to find ways to give tax breaks to the big campaign spenders. The appropriations committees will continue to pump limitless billions into defense while the home districts of committee members stagger happily under the weight of defense contracts and installations. And the highway lobby will continue its efforts to bury the nation under a layer of concrete.

And the taxpayers will pay and pay and pay—and wonder why the more they pay, the less they get. They know they're being had but they don't know how; and they wonder what to do about it. They will keep on wondering until they wake up to their own power—and understand what they must do with that power.

They are going to have to demand that our public process be responsive. They are going to have to demand that our politicians be continuously accountable. They are going to have to insist that the people be given access to their own institutions.

Common Cause intends to help them do just that.

A CONCERN FOR THE PUBLIC INTEREST

To achieve the necessary changes, Common Cause often finds itself in an adversary position toward politicians. But we are not antagonistic to them. We care enough about the political process to want to make it better.

We respect the party system—more than we respect the parties at this moment in their history. We care enough about it to want to see the parties come to life. We want the parties to be responsive to their own rank-and-file members. And we're going to give them trouble until they respond.

We respect representative government. We want to

make it work. We don't want to substitute Common Cause for the representatives of the people. We want the representatives of the people to live up to their high mission. And we're going to keep after them until they do.

We know the role we want to play. As citizens, we intend to pursue the old American custom of saying to our public servants, "Shape up!"

We do not regard ourselves as speaking from some morally superior vantage point "outside the system." We are also a part of "the system." Most of us are members of one of the major parties. Some hold political office. Many are involved in special-interest groups—labor, business, the professions.

What we share is a concern for the public interest. We share a recognition that no one of us will prosper for long if the community deteriorates. If the nation fails, we all fail.

And we share the conviction that as citizens we have every right to raise hell when we see injustice done, or the public interest betrayed, or the public process corrupted.

The chapters that follow do not offer a grand design for solving the nation's problems. They offer first steps —but important first steps—that will bring us to a point where we can again begin to function effectively as a nation.

I shall try to explain why citizen action is needed, and what some of the targets of that action must be. I shall describe the nature and role of citizen action in our society. And I shall describe—against that background— the emergence of Common Cause.

CHAPTER ONE

Politics and Government

THIS BOOK IS an account of some significant things the citizen can do if he puts his mind to it. It is a hopeful statement if you believe, as I do, that he can be persuaded to put his mind to it. But before we reach the hopeful theme of citizen action, we must talk about some grim realities.

THE INTERLOCKING REVOLUTIONS

As citizens observing the national scene, we become so absorbed in the details of domestic policy and current political leadership that we underestimate the dimensions of what we are going through. To comprehend the scope of our difficulties requires a broader canvas.

As a nation, as a species, as inhabitants of this planet, we are caught up in deep and massive changes over which we have limited control. The revolutions in transportation, communications, and sources of energy continue to rock our world and reshape it. The computer revolution is just beginning, but it promises changes at least as startling as the older revolutions.

The biological revolution is also just beginning—and in the long run may prove to be the most unsettling of all. It has already produced spectacular changes in one of man's oldest technologies—agriculture. It has produced methods of birth control that are of profound importance to our future. It has yielded antibiotics, new pesticides (with good and bad consequences), growth-producing hormones, organ transplants, and the possibility of intervention in the processes of heredity.

In a class by itself is the swift evolution of new weapons of war—weapons that could bring the whole human enterprise to a halt.

Along with these scientific and technological revolutions has come the emergence of new political weapons, and an increasing demand for self-determination on the part of hitherto subordinated people.

THE STRAIN ON INSTITUTIONS

In short, we are dealing with a series of interlocking revolutions. Each in itself is epoch-making. Taken together, their consequences defy human imagination. But of one consequence we are quite certain. The interlocking revolutions have put an almost unbearable strain on our social institutions. All over the world we see the disintegration of traditional social patterns. Once-coherent village cultures have been shattered by the impact of transportation and communication. Once-secure religious communities have undergone profound upheavals. Accepted beliefs have lost their hold; old loyalties have been diluted; old boundaries and bonds of brotherhood have been shattered.

·eakdown of established patterns
of viable new ones. We see a
challenge and change. Yet we
institutions that stubbornly resist
ather than change, or change
f violence. We are plunging
future, dragging with us the
s, and institutional apparatus
of a w...　　　ng. The consequences in loss
of shared pri...　　　pose, in social and individual
breakdown, in sh...　　...., are apparent to all.

Social institutions .. ... renewal. A high proportion of
history's significant chan... s may be attributed to nothing short of disaster—invasions, plagues, famine, and
civil war. The question for us is how to bring about required changes without the stimulus of disaster.

FUEL FOR A CONSTRUCTIVE MOVEMENT

A dangerous and perplexing element in our
situation is the degree to which citizens have lost confidence in their institutions and the leadership of those
institutions. Louis Harris reported recently that the number of Americans who express "a great deal of confidence" in our military leaders showed a drop of 54
percent between 1966 and 1971. In the same five-year
period, those who expressed a great deal of confidence
in our congressional leaders dropped 52 percent; in
leaders of banks and financial institutions, 54 percent;
in leaders of major companies, 50 percent.

Somewhat earlier a Roper survey asked, "Do you feel
that things in this country are generally going in the
right direction today, or do you feel that things have

25

pretty seriously gotten off on the wrong track?" The responses were:

Right direction	23 percent
Wrong track	64 percent
No opinion	13 percent

And shortly after the appearance of the Harris survey mentioned above, the Social Research Center (University of Michigan) reported that between 1964 and 1970 the percentage of adult Americans who expressed a "high degree of trust in the government" dropped from 52 percent to 37 percent. The same study found that those who believe that government wastes a lot of the money we pay in taxes rose from 42 percent to almost 70 percent. Those who think the government is "run for the benefit of all the people," rather than for the benefit of a few big interests, dropped from 73 percent to 41 percent.

No serious observer can read the results of these surveys without uneasiness. The statistics are a prescription for social disaster. When citizens cease to have confidence in their own institutions, the nation is in trouble.

When one sees massive shifts in opinion of the sort recorded in these surveys one knows that the people involved do not constitute merely a political fringe or a margin of malcontents. One is dealing with a startling shift in attitude on the part of large numbers of middle-class Americans who would not normally describe themselves as dissenters.

Anyone who travels about this country will obtain ample evidence confirming the survey results. The average citizen is troubled and restive. The feeling is virtually universal that the institutions that should be serving us are not serving us. Citizens at every level and in every

26

the ghetto resident. All are baffled as to how they can cope with the invisible processes that govern their lives.

The loss of confidence in our institutions isn't a visible, objective reality like a flood or a recession. One might more easily compare it to the unmeasurable subterranean stresses that precede a major earthquake. The fact that those stresses are not easily measured makes each major quake a shattering surprise. We must not ignore the possibility of such shattering surprises on the political and social front—indeed, we've already had a few.

As people feel increasingly powerless, the level of social responsibility in the society drops precipitously. It's hard to feel socially responsible when one feels unconnected and anonymous—and evidence that citizens feel that way is overwhelming. So too is the increasing evidence of irresponsibility.

The surest cure for social irresponsibility is to give people something to be responsible about, to give them a significant role in the functioning of the community.

THE RESTIVE MIDDLE

The University of Michigan study reported some especially significant data on the change that has occurred in the middle range of American opinion. Believing that the Vietnam war might have had something to do with the results of their study, the researchers calculated separate scores for those who supported our role in the war, those who opposed it, and the moderates in between. The results were surprising.

	Percentage of those expressing a high degree of confidence in the government.	
	1964	*1970*
Those supporting our role	54	41
Those opposing	60	44
Moderates	74	26

The most striking loss of confidence occurred among the moderates.

On this and other issues, the "alienation of the middle" is more portentous than the riots and bombs through which radical groups express their discontent. The middle is that part of the political spectrum that sets the nation on a new course. Radicals and prophets may see it coming and prepare the way for it. But nothing profound happens until the middle is ready.

It is rarely ready. It is usually complacent, inert, preoccupied with the routines of life, embedded in the *status quo*.

Today the middle is ready. For something. It could be something very good or something very bad.

The loss of confidence constitutes an explosive charge that could splinter our major parties. It could lead us to follow the shallowest of demagogues. It could result in massive refusals to vote. It could lead to increasing violence or to severe repressive measures. But the same electric charge might be the fuel for a truly constructive movement. The very depth and breadth of our concern means that many people are ready to act constructively even if it means sacrifice.

would fight and die for the principle of self-government neglect the instruments of self-government. Americans have always been proud of the opening words of the Preamble to the Constitution: "We, the people of the United States . . ." Yet most of us no longer act in that spirit of personal involvement.

Too high a percentage of Americans avoid political action or think of themselves as above politics. They complain about the inefficiency and corruption of state and local government but take no steps to make it better. They say neither party nominates candidates of real stature, but few of them participate in steps to reshape the party machinery. Earlier generations fought to give us freedom of the ballot, yet only 43 percent of eligible voters went to the polls in the November 1970 elections. Reformers struggled for years to establish the direct primary as a substitute for boss rule, yet the vote in most primaries is small. Most state legislatures are riddled with corruption, yet the citizen has tolerated them.

Among the democracies of the world, our country ranks far from the top in voter participation.

- Sixty-five percent of American voters don't vote regularly.
- Half can't name their congressman, and 65 percent can't name both of their senators.
- Eighty-six percent are unable to identify anything their congressman has ever done; 96 percent cannot identify any policy he stands for.

29

The citizen excuses himself with a cynical comment on politics. But no excuse can conceal the fact that what he is neglecting are the processes of self-government.

Critics of this free society charge that the system has failed us. All the evidence indicates that we are failing the system. The circumstance is tragic, not just because the system needs the citizen, but because the citizen would feel less frustrated if he were participating.

If our Founding Fathers returned today, few things would surprise them more than the citizen's neglect of politics and government, particularly in view of our professed concern for individual freedom. For Jefferson and his contemporaries, the connection was elementary: nothing could be clearer than that liberty and justice for the individual could come *only* from suitably designed instruments of self-government. In their view, a concern for freedom and an interest in government were inseparable. The first business of free men was governing.

That thought would never occur to most Americans today. And we are paying for our thoughtlessness. Out of thousands of years of experience in domesticating the savagery of human conflict and conflicting human purposes, man has distilled law and government and politics. As citizens, we honor law—or at least we have until recently. But we neglect government. And too many of us scorn politics. No wonder we're in trouble.

It is precisely in the political forum that free citizens can have their say, trade out their differences, and identify their shared purposes. Where else, how else can a free people orchestrate their inevitably conflicting purposes?

I am not proposing that we enlarge an already unwieldy government apparatus. I am proposing that we cope with some abuse of the public interest in the private sector, such as the exploitation of the consumer, they generally have to turn to government. And government generally fails them miserably.

We must restore the confidence of our people in their institutions. That means, inevitably, making the institutions worthy of their confidence.

Ineffective government may be advantageous to some Americans, but is is not advantageous to most citizens. People at the middle and lower economic levels of the society, who have relatively few privileges when the society is working well, are subject to even greater and more persistent hardships when government fails.

When the city decays, the prosperous American moves to the suburbs. When the system of justice breaks down, he hires a high-priced lawyer. When the public schools fail, he sends his children to expensive private schools. He can buy an escape from almost any discomfort or trouble. But when the common man looks around for some instruments to accomplish what *he* wants accomplished, he has to turn to the instruments of self-government. They are *his* instruments. Or should be. He had better make them work.

They are not working today. At least, they're not working for him.

One of the gravest aspects of the situation is that the inadequacies of government make it impossible for good men and women to be effective in public life. The system smothers them, thwarts them, chews them up. Contrary to the popular impression, good people do go into politics and government. I have seen them go into Congress, into city councils, into state legislatures, and the results are depressing. Too often they find themselves hamstrung, caught in antiquated institutions that cannot be made to work. And if good people in politics and government are frustrated, good people outside are less likely to come in.

A CONSTITUENCY FOR CHANGE

Skeptics say, "But you can't really change such things." Nonsense! Almost everything about our political and governmental system has evolved and changed continuously in the past. The political parties have evolved in striking ways since the birth of the Republic. The Congress of the United States has changed in dramatic ways since its founding. The Executive Branch has been transformed in even more striking ways. Why should we assume now that the public process has lost its capacity for further change.

Most, if not all, of the solutions proposed in the following pages have been recommended over and over by serious citizens. But there has been no active, powerful, hard-hitting constituency to fight for those solutions. It is the purpose of Common Cause to provide such a constituency.

and Purchase

MOST of the political process has be-
come, behind the scenes, a vast game of barter and purchase involving campaign contributions, appointments
to high office, business favors, favorable legal decisions,
favorable location of defense installations. It is a game
that is going on all the time at every level of government.
And it is paid for, ultimately, by you and me.

It is not easy to describe that behind-the-scenes game
without seeming to condemn more of the political process than one intends, or to indict the good politicians
along with the bad. The game includes activities that
range from outright criminality to legitimate (though
foxy) political deals. We must not be patronizing about
the latter. Politics is, among other things, a trading out
of conflicting interests; and even honest traders are apt
to explore the permissible limits of adroitness. A society
that does not want conflicting interests resolved by the
edict of a tyrant, and does not want opposing elements
to draw guns, will honor its professional conciliators—
chief among them, its politicians.

Unfortunately, however, the game of barter and purchase has gone far, far beyond acceptable limits; the

public interest is sacrificed far too readily and far too often; and the citizen must understand better than he does now the multiplicity of ways in which his interests are compromised. He knows that politics has its seamy side; but he doesn't know how enormous that seamy side really is. Nor does he know what a high percentage of his tax dollar goes to support it.

Even where our government is functioning most effectively, as in the best-managed federal agencies, we have allowed the public interest to be seriously endangered by the trading of political favors. In our less effective institutions—meaning most of them—we have seriously impaired the public process with political wheeling and dealing and the spirit of the commercial transaction.

POLITICAL FAVORS

Armed with the power and money we give them with our votes and tax dollars, politicians are well equipped to play their part in the cycle of favors and obligations. And there is no end to the ways in which they can favor their friends and allies.

States, counties, and cities must bank their money. This runs to vast sums and generally draws no interest. One study estimates that by not collecting the normal interest on such accounts, the federal government subsidizes commercial banks to the extent of $3 to $4 billion a year—which is money out of the taxpayer's pocket. Since bank rates are uniform, competitive bidding is out of the question and political favoritism often dominates the selection of those banks that are to receive government deposits.

Every level of government uses private insurance companies, and the policies involved may be enormous.

THE GAME OF BARTER AND PURCHASE

As in the case of banks, insurance rates are uniform and there is no possibility of competitive bidding, so political factors often weigh heavily.

Every level of government buys or leases large quantities of goods and services—paper clips and patrol cars, office furniture and computers, food, medicine, street lights; and issues franchises to private business —to run cafeterias in public buildings, operate bus lines, place vending machines on government property, run newsstands. Personal fortunes have been made through the capacity to win such favors from the party in power.

Every level of government has enormous favors to hand out in grants and contracts. The selection of a developer for an urban renewal contract may mean millions for the firm involved.

At all levels of government, acquisition or disposal of real estate and construction of government buildings bring juicy profits to real estate men, fat commissions to architects, and huge sums for the "in" contractors.

The attorney general, senators, governors, mayors, and party leaders all have something to say in the handing out of judgeships. While the federal judiciary holds to generally high standards, judgeships at lower levels are sometimes sold for cash on the barrelhead and many are bartered for political loyalty and past or future favors. Judges in their turn hand out lucrative favors. They have it in their power to appoint receivers, guardians, trustees, referees, appraisers. The fees for the trustee in a complex bankruptcy case may run to hundreds of thousands of dollars. When a guardian is appointed by the court to protect the interest of an infant heir, the fee is often based on the size of the estate rather than the work done. The man appointed as appraiser of the value of an estate may collect a fat fee for virtually no work.

As for the classic form of patronage, jobs, there are

not only the top-level appointments that hit the head-lines, but countless jobs in parks, playgrounds, the sanitation department, hospitals, sewers, jails, and courts. Some governors (e.g., the governor of Pennsylvania) and mayors (e.g., the mayor of Chicago) have tens of thousands of jobs at their disposal. A 1962 study showed that fully 46 percent of full-time city employees were excluded from civil service. The attorney general of the United States has a particularly powerful patronage network because of the importance of the posts at his disposal—U.S. attorneys, assistant U.S. attorneys, marshals and judges.

Mayors and local party leaders generally control the issuance of business permits, which means they can delay, prevent, or facilitate the opening of new businesses. They can secure tax abatement for an industry that is friendly. And they can arrange zoning variances—a particularly rich source of profit to real estate interests close to the party in power.

Government attorneys (or their supervisors) can forego prosecution of those who are close to the reigning political powers. As the Lord tempers the wind to the shorn lamb, the politician lightens retribution to the fat cat.

The President's capacity to reward his friends is immeasurable. Simply by the level at which he sets an item in the budget he can alter the outlook for an entire industry. By resisting or endorsing regulatory legislation, he can transform the environment in which thousands of firms do business. He can rescue an airline from the edge of bankruptcy with a favorable route award. He can delay or quash antitrust action where it affects his friends.

Of all the favors government can bestow, none is more succulent than the tax break. And of all groups that have benefited by that form of largesse, none has

been more adroit and more greedy than the oil industry. The 27.5 percent oil depletion allowance that prevailed until 1969 deprived the Treasury of more than a billion dollars a year in taxes. President Truman said, "I know of no loophole so inequitable." In 1969 it was pared down to 22 percent, still an extraordinary tax break for an industry that ranks second only to pharmaceuticals in profitability. Some notion of the financial stakes involved may be seen from the fact that Atlantic Richfield earned $797 million in net income in the years from 1962 through 1968, yet paid *no* federal tax in the first six years of that period and only 1.2 percent in the seventh year.

WHAT FLOWS THE OTHER WAY?

With all that flood of favors pouring out from the politicians, what flows in the other direction? The answer is "money." The powerful and pervasive influence of money in politics is the "dirty little secret" that everybody knows. Today it usually changes hands in the form of campaign contributions. In Indiana they are very matter-of-fact about it and require that every patronage employee contribute 2 percent of his salary to the party machine. And that arrangement is only slightly more explicit than the universal practice. When the campaign begins the party money-raisers go down their list of "friends"—the architect who received a commission for the new customs house, the bank that benefited heavily from government deposits, the insurance company that profits from a huge policy, the wealthy developer who was tapped for the urban renewal program, the industry that received a tax break involving billions. And the "friends" pay off.

Thus is the public interest bought and sold. No wonder we have so many moral midgets in the seats of the mighty.

Only very impatient or stupid men give or take cash bribes any more. It is dreadfully old-fashioned. The preferred mode of corruption today is either the campaign gift or circuitous and hard-to-trace business favors. The businessman who receives a favor from a legislative committee chairman may buy all his personal insurance from the company in which that chairman has a financial interest. The union that has received favors from a member of Congress may throw its legal business to the law firm in which the congressman retains his partnership. In short, the *quid pro quo* may not go directly to the official who did the favor, but to a relative, to a company in which he has stock, to a law firm with which he is still associated. It is almost impossible to link such actions to the original favor. A company is free to choose its law firm. If it happens to choose the firm whose most distinguished partner is the chairman of a powerful congressional committee, that is hardly a crime.

It is all very civilized. And low-keyed. And polite. So much so that people raise their eyebrows when one calls it corruption. But some of us are just simple-minded enough to believe that when public policy is bent in a particular direction as a result of financial favors done to the policy-maker, that is corruption, embroider it how you will.

The potentialities for corruption based on campaign spending have increased greatly due to the soaring costs of the political campaign. In 1968, according to the best available estimates, $100 million was spent on the Presidential campaigns and $200 million more on all other election campaigns. The total was up 50 percent over 1964. In the congressional elections of 1970 a number of senators spent in the neighborhood of $1 million on their campaigns, and a number of representatives spent up to $250,000.

There are people who give to political campaigns out of honest conviction, and honest politicians who receive campaign gifts. But most political giving is done with the intent to buy influence. Former Senator Albert Gore said, ". . . Any person who is willing to sell his soul can have handsome financing for his campaigns." And Senator Russell Long said in 1967, "Investments in this area can be viewed as monetary bread cast upon the water to be returned a thousandfold." *

A thousandfold sounds like excessive return on an investment, but the senator was not exaggerating as much as one might think. The campaign contributions in a Presidential election year run to a few hundred million. The return flow of political favors to donors must be reckoned in the scores of billions. And it's the taxpayer's money. Oil import quotas alone cost the American consumer an estimated $7.2 billion a year.

Corporations are not allowed to contribute to political campaigns, but they resort to innumerable devices to channel contributions through their employees. Some pay their officers cash bonuses, a portion of which the officer is expected to contribute to the political slush fund. One employee said in a sworn statement that he was told to contribute $1,200 and instructed to "recover the amount by covering it up in [his] traveling expense account." Some corporations provide salary supplements with the same understanding. Some allow the candidate

---

* The comment was made in the course of a speech on the Senate floor. The speech stands as the most candid indictment of uncontrolled campaign financing ever made by any senator, let alone a Senate Establishmentarian such as Long. He was urging that the individual taxpayer be permitted to earmark $1 of his income tax payment for a presidential election campaign fund.

to pile up huge bills (airline, hotel, etc.) and then write them off as uncollectable.

Another threat to the public interest is the widespread conflicts of interest in which a public official has a personal financial stake in the very matters on which he is legislating. Such conflicts are all too common among legislators at both state and federal levels. In Congress, at last count, there were ninety-five members of the House of Representatives who had a personal investment in a bank or other financial institution, thirty-seven of them being on the board of directors of the institution in question. The Ways and Means Committee, which passes on legislation of crucial importance to financial institutions, has seven members who themselves have a personal financial investment in such institutions; and the Banking and Currency Committee has seven more.

Law ranks second as an outside interest. At least fifty-seven members of the House, including eleven from its Judiciary Committee, are still actively associated with a law firm, or continuing some sort of individual practice.

The Senate probably has a comparable record, but Senators are required to reveal almost nothing of their private business connections, so we cannot know for sure.

DETERIORATION OF THE PUBLIC PROCESS

It would have been easy to liven the preceding pages with lurid case histories of corruption—the conviction of Bobby Baker in the early 1960s for income tax evasion and conspiracy to defraud the government;

the conviction in 1970 of Speaker McCormack's aide, Martin Sweig, for perjury in a case the judge described as involving "corruption of a very profound kind," and so on. The examples are plentiful and colorful. But such notorious cases do not make the appropriate point. There will always be rascals. The point is that deals counter to the public interest are an everyday occurrence at every level of government: little deals, big deals, outright criminality by shady characters, suave betrayals of trust by distinguished officials.

No sensible person expects politics to reflect an antiseptic rationality. Politicians must reconcile conflicting interests, must be skilled in compromise, must win loyal allies among widely differing groups. Men and women who are facile in such difficult arts will not always use their facility scrupulously. Politics will always be somewhat earthy. But there are tolerable limits, and we have left those limits light-years behind us.

Corruption in American politics is nothing new. But today, when no citizen can fully comprehend the involuted workings of our huge and complex society, it is easier for corruption to flourish and spread like an invisible cancer. And it is in important ways more offensive to the citizen today. In the nineteenth century, a populace held together by powerful shared values and riding an exhilarating wave of national confidence could look somewhat tolerantly on corrupt politics. Today, with our shared values disintegrating and all our institutions experiencing a crisis of confidence, we are in no mood for tolerance.

It is not just the individual citizen who is hurt by the shady side of political barter and purchase. The nation is hurt when great decisions are made by venal men, concerned chiefly with private gain, the payment

41

of political obligations, or the consolidation of personal power,

Consider the courts. When, in the selection of a judge, competence becomes irrelevant, as it has in many cases, and party loyalty the only criterion of appointment; when the men chosen are so obligated politically that they are not independent agents; when the system operates on the assumption that they will favor political cronies in the courtroom; and when the court personnel below the level of judge are selected on the same basis— undeviating loyalty with no test of competence—then the whole system becomes a joke.

But it isn't a joke for the average citizen who finds himself in court. The prosperous American hires an expensive lawyer to ensure that his interests do not get lost in the morass of a broken-down system. But the citizen of average income is on his own in a sea of incompetence and unconcern.

The disintegrating effect of corruption goes beyond the specific decisions made. The uninhibited play of backroom politics is antagonistic to clarity of public policy; behind-the-scenes bartering proceeds with greatest freedom in the total absence of clear policy.

Administrative confusion is an advantageous environment for buyers and sellers of political influence—but it is a fatal environment for effective government. Sound public policy cannot be formulated. Programs cannot be well administered. The public process falls apart.

When political and governmental institutions are eaten out and corroded by deals and favoritism, they finally deteriorate to the point where they can't serve anybody.

The question is how long the hardworking, law-abiding, tax-paying American is going to put up with it. How long?

TIME TO END THE FLIM-FLAM

One of the most moving lines in the Declaration of Independence appears at the very end of that document. In support of the Declaration, the signers say, ". . . we mutually pledge to each other our lives, our fortunes, and our sacred honor." Down the years, many Americans have followed them in that pledge. We have had our full share of rascals and cynics in American history, but we have also had our share of those who gave their lives, literally and figuratively, to make this nation a model for all mankind. They believed the words of the Declaration. They not only pledged but gave their lives, their fortunes, and their sacred honor. All to what end? To create government with a "For Sale" sign on it?

Perhaps at a less critical time in our history we could tolerate rascality in high places. But not now. Our country is in deep trouble. We cannot tolerate the dominance of courthouse politics, the shady deal and the crass payoff. It is time for the citizen to stand up and say "Enough!" It is time to end the flim-flam and put our political institutions into working order. It can be done.

CHAPTER THREE

Access

In THE LATE 1960s the phrase "power to the people" became a fashionable radical slogan. And those who shouted it seemed somehow to imagine that the "power" they sought had been left lying around in the streets, waiting to be gathered in by demonstrators. They seemed not to understand that those who benefit by the present distribution of power have skillfully built their privileges and prerogatives into our laws, our institutional arrangements, and our customary ways of doing business. Anyone concerned to strengthen the hand and voice of the people must have the patience to understand the arrangements by which the present inequitable distribution of power is preserved.

If the citizen is to regain command of his political institutions, he must begin at the beginning. And the beginning is "access"—the citizen's access to his political and governmental institutions. As we shall see, he has been deprived of that access by the skillful, deliberate, and systematic use of two instruments—money and secrecy.

The two most important forms of access are *adequate information* and *a means of participating:* the right to know and the right to have one's say.

Access is desirable not only for its value to democracy,

but because it insures the vitality of institutions. Leaders always need corrective signals from the levels at which their institutions touch living reality—the grass roots, the operating level, the front lines. When an organization becomes so huge and sprawling that the decision-maker never sees the consequences of his decisions decay sets in rapidly. Even a nondemocratic institution (e.g., a giant corporation) suffers when the men at the top receive too little feedback from the grass-roots. One of the reasons monopolistic firms go to seed is that people have to use the goods or services whether they are satisfied or not, so that one major form of feedback—the rising or falling sales curve—has been rendered meaningless.

INSIDERS' GAMES

Access seems such an obvious social good, how could anyone possibly be against it? Unfortunately, it seems almost easier to be against it than for it. From the dawn of history, all human institutions have tended over time to become insiders' games. An institution, no matter how high-minded, tends more and more to fall into the hands of an inside clique. Increasingly effective barriers are erected to prevent those outside the circle of power from influencing decisions. One could name any number of American cities that are in fact run behind the scenes by a small group of insiders—some of them elected, most of them not. The reader can supply examples out of his own experience with corporations, universities, churches, clubs, the armed services.

Though it seems like a realistic game for the insiders involved, it is in fact a very impractical way to keep institutions alive and vital. It contributes enormously to their early decay. Inexorably, the time arrives when the

45

insiders against save own themselves. And they don't know why. They can't bring themselves to face the fact that they have shut themselves off from the new blood and fresh ideas and cross-currents of criticism that would rejuvenate the institution.

The tendency of institutions to become insiders' games is illustrated all too clearly in our municipal and state governments, our political parties, our Congress, and our federal agencies. The typical political unit is not designed in such a way that the revitalizing currents of public concern will affect it deeply. Quite the contrary. It is designed so that various special interests working behind the scenes can shape the course of events almost without reference to public opinion.

There is no better example than the functioning of the House Ways and Means Committee, which shapes the laws governing every tax dollar that we pay. After the committee concludes public hearings, its business sessions are secret and are dominated by the chairman and the ranking minority (Republican) member. The members of the committee are not allowed to bring even their own staff assistants to the secret meetings, so they are denied the expert advice that might make them effective independent voices in the committee. Procedures are informal, based on consensus, so votes are rarely taken. When the legislation (fashioned chiefly by the chairman and the ranking Republican) comes to the floor of the House, it comes under a closed rule and is always passed. The closed rule means that no member of the House can offer an amendment to the bill. This is why—to mention only one example—there has never been a direct House vote on the highly controversial oil depletion allowance.

If the reader has any question of the power of the Ways and Means Committee Chairman to hand out or withhold favors to special interests behind that cloak of secrecy, he would do well to look up a news dispatch by David Broder to the *Washington Post* dated March 1, 1972. The dispatch reported that among those braving the snows of New Hampshire to campaign for Wilbur Mills for President were a lobbyist for Japanese and European textile firms, a lobbyist for banking and insurance interests, a utilities lobbyist, and a legislative agent for the Gas Supply Committee. Contemplating that sort of thing, even the least cynical of citizens may begin to discern—as the saying goes—the footprints of a hidden hand. One of the lobbyists, Michael Daniels, a registered foreign agent of the Embassy of Japan, explained his presence in New Hampshire by saying, "Mr. Mills is a personal friend of mine." Affection runs deep in Washington.

INFORMATION

All democratic theory assumes that the citizen must first of all be informed. But it's difficult to hold to that standard. Much that the individual needs to know to be a better citizen (or a better consumer) is either extremely technical or imperceptible to the naked eye. The citizen can't judge for himself how much lead is being spewed into the air from auto exhausts, or whether a new drug has dangerous side effects. He cannot understand the complex workings of federal, state, and local governments.

Unfortunately, few government or private agencies have set themselves the task of clarifying things for the citizen or gathering and disseminating the kinds of basic information the citizen would have to have to be an effective voice.

47

Far from helping the citizen to be informed, many (perhaps most) governmental and corporate institutions suppress information. Much of the business of Congress is still conducted in secret. Both the revenue and appropriations committees of both houses hold their business sessions behind closed doors. State legislatures are even less willing to do the public business publicly; some of them operate virtually as secret societies. Regulatory agencies often function behind closed doors, suppress reports the public should see, omit public hearings, and refuse to give out data that might reflect unfavorably on the business concerns they are regulating.

Private sector institutions show the same penchant for secrecy. When Congress began moving to cope with secret Swiss bank accounts,* not only did domestic banks fail to endorse the congressional effort, some domestic banks made it clear that they coveted the same secrecy for their own branches in Switzerland. Fortunately, Congress paid them little heed.

Utilities and common carriers often raise their rates without adequate warning—and the regulatory body is often an accomplice in the secrecy. Pharmaceutical companies have often suppressed reports of adverse medical findings on drugs. Industries have blocked the release of government reports that reflected unfavorably on their product.

We shall remedy none of these evils until we launch a sustained attack on government behind closed doors. To tear away the veil of secrecy, we must have "freedom of information" and "open meetings" statutes in every state of the Union and in the federal government.†

---

* According to one informed estimate, in the four years from 1966 to 1970, 5 billion dollars in U.S. money was deposited in secret Swiss accounts to evade U.S. income taxes.

† The federal government already has a freedom of information statute but it is in urgent need of strengthening.

Such statutes should cover both legislative and executive branches of government and should require that the public business be done publicly. Executive agencies should be required to make available to the public any information that is not vital to the nation's security or an invasion of individual privacy. There should be remedies available to the citizen if information is withheld.

Legislative bodies should conduct their affairs openly and record their votes; there should be public hearings, announced well in advance, on all significant legislation. There should be an open record of committee deliberations. There should be open party caucuses. All legislators should send their voting records regularly to their constituents, and hometown newspapers should publish such information.

Regulatory bodies must require that the industries they regulate provide adequate information on which the consumer can base judgments, expressed in terms the consumer can understand. And the agency itself should gather the kind of data that will inform the citizen.

THE IMAGE MANIPULATORS

A wholly different problem is the use of modern communications techniques with the deliberate intent of misleading or misinforming the citizen on political matters. The grossest example is provided by the use during election campaigns of the television spot-announcement of sixty seconds or less. The brief spot-announcement, in the hands of unscrupulous campaign managers, is image manipulation at its worst.

The aim of the new approach is *not* to make the voter think, *not* to clarify the issues, *not* to give him a greater grasp of his role as a citizen *or* a deeper understanding of the candidate. The aim is to sell him an illusion, to move him to act without thinking, to con him psychologically.

The essence of the new approach is to remove from public view as completely as possible the real flesh-and-blood candidate—that anachronistic soul who dashed around meeting honest-to-God people, answering questions, debating real issues, letting himself be seen and heard and judged as a human being. Most of our candidates still follow that traditional pattern, at the same time that they are experimenting with the newer techniques. But the more candid of the new-style political managers make no bones about the "inefficiency" of the old-style dash-about candidate. Not until he is safely removed can the modern political manager proceed with the carefully contrived image which he will project over the electronic media. As one cynical operator put it to me, "Given today's techniques, the best way to handle the candidate is to lock him in a broom closet. Let him out occasionally, apply the makeup, rehearse him in some easy dialogue and run him through a TV spot. Then—back to the closet."

The political announcement running sixty seconds or less is too brief for discussion of any significant issue. It is in fact a studied means of *not* informing the voter in any significant way. Common Cause has urged political candidates to insist that any television material produced for their campaigns be at least five minutes in length. They should appear live or in unedited sequences. They should expose themselves to unrehearsed dialogue and questioning.

One major television station and two advertising firms have said that they will have nothing to do with the political announcement of sixty seconds or less. But others do not appear to be following their lead.

If broadcasters and candidates continue to use the

brief TV spots, one alternative remains. Let the viewer tune them out. Or walk away from them. Or laugh at them as one would laugh at an old-fashioned carnival snake-oil pitchman. We must free ourselves from the slick, technologically crafted political lie.

FREEDOM OF THE MEDIA

None of the activities we have talked about—informing the citizen, enabling him to participate, providing him with skilled advocacy—can possibly work without freedom of information. The two continuing threats to freedom of the media are governmental and commercial.

Government intimidation of the media is not likely to take the form of straightforward censorship. Government intervention, if it comes, will be infinitely more subtle and dangerous. Just as the government can do favors for those in its good graces, so it can intimidate those who are not. It can revoke licenses. It can go over tax returns with a fine-tooth comb. It can block moves such as mergers or acquisitions that require government approval. In short, it can make life difficult.

This is something that every owner of a newspaper or television station knows by heart. So when members of the administration attack the media, no one takes them lightly. Some owners inevitably move toward the kinds of accommodation that will put them more in line with the administration point of view. Such government pressure, stepped up and maintained over time, could produce profound changes in the atmosphere surrounding the gathering, reporting, and interpreting of news.

The other threat to freedom of the media is the influence of commercial interests. On March 7, 1972, the

51

New York Times reported that Bumble Bee Seafoods had withdrawn its advertising from CBS "to penalize" the CBS network for its coverage of Senator Philip Hart's investigation of the fishing inspection bill.

One major network (NBC) which must report objectively on defense matters, e.g., the value of a new weapons system, is owned by a corporation (RCA) with heavy defense contracts.

The *Journal of the American Medical Association,* which should scrutinize new drugs with a cold eye, derives approximately half of its income from advertising —primarily drug advertising.

A particularly serious threat lies in the increasingly centralized control of newspapers, TV and radio stations. In 1910 the cities and towns with daily newspapers under two or more separate ownerships numbered 57.1 percent of the total. By 1930, it had dropped to 21.5 percent. By 1970, it was 4.13 percent. Today, 1,483 cities have monopoly ownerships and 64 have competing ownerships. Newspaper chains have grown steadily. Linked ownership of newspapers, TV stations, and radio stations has increased.

Even more troubling is the fact that news outlets are coming increasingly into the hands of conglomerates which are deeply involved in businesses unrelated to the information field. How honestly will media thus controlled report news that might do commercial injury to the other parts of the conglomerate? Will a radio station owned by AVCO Corporation, one of the largest defense contractors in the country, report objectively on military expenditure controversies? Will the Wilmington, Delaware, newspapers owned by Christiana Securities report accurately on matters affecting E. I. Dupont de Nemours and Company, of whose stock it owns 27 percent?

We must frame statutes that prohibit linked owner-ship of newspapers, TV and radio stations in the same metropolitan area; and that prevent ownership of media by unrelated business interests (and vice versa).

THE OPPORTUNITY TO PARTICIPATE

The other ingredient of access is the opportunity to participate. Like the "right to know," it is a principle more honored in commencement speeches than in daily practice. In a democracy, the central means of participating is the ballot, and there is a long, shameful record of deliberately erected barriers to voting. The worst of such barriers have been eliminated, thanks to the Voting Rights Act of 1965, but there are still unnecessary difficulties in registration.

In most states the process by which candidates get on the ballot, i.e., the nominating process, has all too often been one to which the citizen has had no access at all. As recently as 1968, in most states, the rank-and-file party member—Republican or Democrat—had little or nothing to do with selecting or instructing his own delegates to the national convention of his own party. It was done, in most states, in the back room.

The citizen doesn't have to put up with that. The years from 1968 to 1972 saw important beginnings in opening up delegate selection for the national conventions, at least in the Democratic Party. In December 1971, Common Cause distributed to its members detailed descriptions of the delegate selection process in each of the fifty states, so that the members could understand the process and participate in it if they wished.

For other than Presidential elections, unfortunately, nominating procedures are still the most invisible and neglected of political activities.

Another problem of concern to the citizen is that the selection of a Vice Presidential candidate is still done in the back room. The national convention delegates can do little but ratify the individual chosen by their Presidential candidate. And his prime criterion in choosing a running mate is not the suitability of the man to succeed to the Presidency.

All Presidential candidates should make public during the primaries, the names of those whom they will consider for Vice President, and to pledge that they will recommend to their party conventions only names from this group. This would allow the voters, the media, and convention delegates to weigh the records and views of all potential Vice Presidential candidates. The final decision should be made by the convention delegates, not as a rubber stamp but after serious deliberation on the choices before them. Then when we pray for the President's health it will not be for fear of what the succession might bring.

There are many other points in the public process at which participation is blocked. In many state legislatures and city councils, public hearings on important matters are omitted altogether or held without adequate advance publicity. Most regulatory agencies, both state and federal, give ample access to the industries being regulated but are little inclined to permit citizen intervention. Some years ago, Justice Warren Burger reprimanded both the Federal Communications Commission and the industry for such conduct. He said, "The broadcasting industry does not seem to have grasped the simple fact that a broadcast license is a public trust subject to termination for breach of duty. We cannot believe that the congressional mandate of public participation . . . was meant to be limited to writing letters to the Commission, to inspection of records, to the Commission's grace in considering listener claims, or to mere non-participating appearance at hearings."

THE FULL-THROATED VOICE OF MONEY

But the deepest problem of citizen participation does not stem from the fact that decisions are made behind closed doors. The most serious obstacle the citizen faces when he sets out to participate is that someone with a lot of money got there first and bought up the public address system. The full-throated voice of money drowns him out. It isn't just that money talks. It talks louder and longer and drowns out the citizen's hoarse whisper.

All citizens should have equal access to decision-making processes of government, but money makes some citizens more equal than others. Harold Geneen, whose company committed $400,000 to help finance the 1972 Republican National Convention in San Diego, had no difficulty in discussing his antitrust problems with three cabinet members, three White House aides, five senators, five representatives, and the chairman of the Federal Reserve Board. That is *access*. And any ordinary citizen who tries to set up a comparable schedule of appointments will learn all he needs to know about the influence of money in politics.

If we wish to diminish the power of money to corrupt the public process, we must pass laws to control campaign financing, to control lobbies, and to require full disclosure of conflict of interest on the part of all public officials.

Such legislation should be passed in every state and at the federal level. These are not impossible goals. Such

55

legislation has been drafted. It has been fought for by citizens' groups on many occasions. But it has never been the subject of an all-out national drive by citizens.

It is difficult to emphasize strongly enough how central such measures are to any improvement in our situation. A country proverb says, "If you want to clear the stream, get the hog out of the spring." Our system is being corrupted and compromised by the power of money to dictate political outcomes. The capacity or willingness of the government to find solutions to any of the problems that plague us—inflation, inequitable taxes, unemployment, housing, urban chaos, dirty air and water—is complicated by the commanding power of monied interests to define the problem and set limits to public action.

CAMPAIGN FUNDS

Common Cause began its fight for controls on campaign spending in 1970. Both houses of Congress passed a bill, but the President vetoed it. We resumed the effort in 1971, beginning with a lawsuit directed at both major parties seeking to restrain them from violating the existing laws governing campaign finance.

In February 1972, the President signed into law a new campaign spending law. It contained some important new measures—limits on media spending and provisions for disclosure of monies received and spent by candidates. But it did not provide for an independent elections commission, nor for adequate enforcement powers, nor for a ceiling on contributions. Time will tell whether the legislation is an adequate remedy for a corrosive political evil.

During the campaign of '72, Common Cause proposed that candidates *at all levels of government* pledge themselves to seek further strengthening of campaign financing controls to diminish the scandalous influence of money in politics. Such legislation should include limits on giving, limits on spending, full disclosure provisions, and an enforcement mechanism.

The press can play a crucial role with respect to campaign spending. The disclosure provisions of the 1972 law opened up wholly new possibilities of journalistic coverage. It should not be occasional coverage. When political campaigns are in progress, spending disclosures —and failures to disclose—should be reported as faithfully as the weather.

CONFLICT OF INTEREST

Equally important, if we are to hold elected officials accountable, is an end to the kind of conflict of interest in which a public official has a personal financial stake in the very matters on which he is legislating. Every candidate for public office—at all levels—should declare his support of laws to cope with such conflict of interest. Every elected official should disclose the sources of his income. Members of Congress should sever all ties with their law firms or directorships while in office. If any vote confronts the legislator with a possible financial conflict of interest, he should declare that conflict openly before the vote is taken.

Thomas Jefferson once said, "In questions of power . . . let no more be heard of confidence in man, but bind him down from mischief by the chains of the Constitution." No doubt our legislators are as honest as the

57

generality of men and women—but somehow that isn't very comforting. Let us bind them down from mischief with conflict-of-interest statutes.

PUBLIC ADVOCACY

Unfortunately, even if governmental and corporate institutions opened up the channels of information and participation tomorrow, the citizens' interest would not be preserved. The special interests seeking their advantage in court or Congress or a regulatory agency are represented by exceedingly skilled full-time advocates. Rarely does the public interest enjoy that advantage. Provisions must be made within government for citizen advocacy through ombudsmen, consumers' councils, and similar measures. Outside government there must be a variety of organizations (such as Common Cause, environmental groups, civil rights organizations) prepared to represent the citizen with professional competence.

CHAPTER FOUR

Responsiveness and Accountability

G IVEN an adequate flow of information to the citizen and ample opportunity for participation, the citizen still needs some means of requiring that government be responsive and accountable.

The first point of impact must be legislation. With all the interminable passing of laws to serve the public interest, how is it that we are still so inadequately protected—from threats to our health and safety, from fraud, from shoddy goods, from pollution? The answer is that the laws written to achieve those ends are too often flawed, and the agencies to administer the laws too often ineffective.

Consider first the defects in the laws. Citizens assume that a bill entitled the Clean Air Act is designed to bring them clean air, and when that result doesn't ensue, they can't understand what went wrong. They would understand better if they knew the power and persistence of the industrial interests that do not want such legislation to be effective. Lobbyists representing those interests follow the legislation every step of the way. Having contributed substantially to the campaigns of many of the legislators, they find receptive listeners. If there is no great public support for the legislation, they will attempt to defeat it. But if there is public clamor for effective action, defeat of the legislation might increase the citizen's anger. In that case the lobbyists generally think it wiser to pass a law that looks reassuring but has been weakened at crucial points so that it cannot be administered or enforced. This is much easier than trying to defeat the legislation altogether. Sometimes, if the lobbyist can persuade those drafting the bill to delete, add, or change one single crucial word, he can fatally weaken the bill. Only very knowing students of the public process will understand what happened.

It is not possible to administer a law that is deliberately ambiguous in defining the proscribed activities, or that deliberately exempts ahead of time some of the worst potential offenders, or that deliberately provides weak enforcement provisions. A favorite tactic of the special interests is to urge that enforcement be lodged with the states, which yield even more easily to special interest pressure than does the federal government.

THE LOBBYING CONTROL STATUTE

There are few clearer examples of deliberately defective legislation than the present federal lobbying control statute. It is a sham and a fraud. The Congress of the United States should be ashamed to have such make-believe legislation on the books. The definition of lobbying contained in the law and the reporting requirements are drafted so vaguely that the large and well-heeled special interests have found it easy to understate the lobbying portion of their expenditures or to evade registering altogether.

Common Cause scrupulously reports every penny spent on federal lobbying, with the result that in the last quarter of 1970—when the organization was only four months old, an infant organization struggling to survive —it appeared to be spending twice as much on federal lobbying as any other organization. In the second quarter of 1971 it appeared to be spending five times as much as any other! No lobbying expenditures at all were reported in that period by—to name a few—the American Bankers Association, the American Public Power Association, the National Rifle Association, General Motors, ITT. What kind of game is that?

It would be better to have no legislation at all than for Congress to lend dignity to such a swindle.

Citizens' groups must become far more professional in monitoring legislation as it moves through Congress. The special interests have found it easy to emasculate public interest legislation because citizens have paid little attention to the details of the legislative process.

CONGRESSIONAL REFORM

Equally important, Congress must overhaul its own structure and procedures to make itself more responsive and accountable, and to provide greater citizen access. An essential first step is to abolish the archaic seniority system by which congressional committees select their chairmen. When Common Cause was founded, in 1970, we tackled the seniority system as one of our first battles.

All of the attributes we seek in our political and governmental institutions—access, responsiveness, accountability—are violated or made more difficult of achievement by the seniority system. But what is at issue most directly is accountability. It is almost impossible to call a committee chairman to account when he never has to stand before his fellow party members for re-election.

The seniority system is a custom, not a rule, of Congress. It awards the chairmanship of a committee to a member from the majority party who has served on the committee the longest period of time. There are no criteria of wisdom, integrity, intelligence, leadership, or courage. If the committee member has served on the committee one day longer than other members, he is entitled to be chairman.

Committee chairmen are the imperious rulers of the Congress. Neither the party leaders nor the Speaker of the House nor the President of the United States can tell a chairman what he must do. The practical consequences are known to everyone in or out of Congress who has tried to move that body toward significant social change. Whether working for civil rights or peace or food for the hungry, one all too often encounters a committee chairman who is wholly unresponsive, even to the fellow members of his own party, because their opinions of him cannot affect his grip on power.

The system gives an overwhelming advantage to the elderly members, and makes it nearly impossible for younger men or women to play significant roles or leadership. In the early 1800s Henry Clay served brilliantly as Speaker of the House, beginning at the age of thirty-three. Contrast that with the situation today in which Speaker McCormack recently retired at the age of seventy-nine and the median age of House chairmen is sixty-nine compared with fifty-three for all members of the House. Comparable ages for members of the Senate are sixty-seven for chairmen and fifty-eight for the Senate as a whole. Some men and women are superbly vital in their seventies but others are not. The business world normally expects its executives to retire at sixty-five.

The seniority system throws the weight of congressional power to the one-party states and House districts, since those areas re-elect the same man year after year.

Some candidates from such districts—Republicans as well as Democrats—run for re-election without any opposition in either a primary or general election. And the states and districts that have a healthy two-party system go virtually unrepresented in the power structure of Congress. California, a tumultuously two-party state has not had a chairmanship of a standing committee in the Senate for twenty-four years—though it is the most populous state in the union.

It is time for Congress to adopt principles of majority rule in the selection of committee chairman. Each committee chairman should stand for re-election as chairman at the beginning of each Congress.

When Common Cause decided to work for abolition of the seniority system, a number of friendly Senators and Representatives warned that it was an unpromising issue to choose as the first campaign of Common Cause. They reminded us that proponents of good government had attacked seniority for years without success, and they insisted that everyone was bored with the issue. They said it was too technical, and that we would never get popular attention focused on it.

Despite the gloomy predictions, our nationwide effort to alert the public was successful. There were front-page stories and editorials across the country. The subject was dealt with by the TV networks. Our members flooded their congressmen with letters, telephone calls, and visits. They wrote letters to their local newspapers. As the campaign drew to a close, Senator Gurney of Florida said he couldn't walk into a Rotary Club luncheon without being asked about the seniority system.

What came out of it all was the first crack in the system in decades. The Democrats (who, as the majority party, hold the chairmanships) agreed that any nomination of a chairman may be challenged in the Democratic caucus if a Representative, supported by ten others, requests a separate vote on the nomination. The Republicans (who had less at stake since they hold none of the chairmanships) voted a comparable change.

We did not break the system but we dented it. Like all issues that have to do with final questions of power, this one will have to be the subject of sustained attack.

There are, of course, many other steps that could be taken to improve the functioning of Congress, but I shall not attempt to list them here. If one were to choose a second congressional reform objective, it would be to make further inroads on the secrecy with which Congress still conducts much of its business (see preceding chapter).

EXECUTIVE AGENCIES

Laws must be administered, and even a good law is of little value in the hands of executive agencies that cannot function effectively.

To repair the functioning of the executive agencies, particularly those at the state and local level, will take extraordinary effort and time. Some of the present agencies took years to evolve to their present level of mediocrity and incompetence. It wasn't the work of a day, and it won't be undone in a day. In some cases a rigorous upgrading of staff will be essential. In other cases, reorganization of the agencies and overhaul of its operating procedures will be needed. Nothing can be accomplished if the agency is poorly conceived, its powers undercut by other parts of the executive branch, its jurisdiction artificially restricted or fragmented. Nor can it function effectively if it is consistently undercut by higher levels of government.

Many citizens wonder why such faults can't be corrected in straightforward fashion. If the agency is badly organized, reorganize it! If the staff is weak, strengthen it! If the agency's authority is not adequate, give it a clear mandate!

It sounds simple. But unfortunately there are those who oppose such action. There are always those who are happy with incompetence and confusion that work to their profit. A special-interest lobbyist may have spent years perfecting his knowledge of the present agency organization with all its quirks and foibles, and polishing his friendships with existing decision-makers. He has, so to speak, spent years digging his tunnel into the public treasury, and he doesn't want the vault moved. Similarly, there are senators and representatives who have discovered that they can profit by the administrative confusion of existing arrangements and will oppose any change.

One of the realities that constantly undermines the public interest is the existence, at both federal and state levels, of what might appropriately be called the unholy trinity. It takes many forms, but most typically it consists of an upper-middle-level bureaucrat (say, a bureau chief from one of the cabinet departments), a legislator (say, a member of one of the appropriations committees), and a lobbyist from one of the well-heeled special-interest groups. As a rule, they will have been friends for years. They have gone fishing together. Their wives play bridge together. They have seen Presidents, cabinet members, and governors come and go. Their names are rarely seen in the newspapers. They are a part of the permanent, invisible government. And as the years go by they shape policy in substantial ways.

It always puzzles the outsider that a cabinet member is not master in his own house; and countless journalistic pieces have been written about the stubborn bureaucrat. It isn't that the cabinet member can't win against the stubborn bureaucrat. He can. But he can't win against a bureaucrat in league with a member of the Appropriations Committee and a powerful lobby. In such a battle, the cabinet member may find his appropriations endangered. He may find himself receiving angry letters and telephone calls from a variety of influential people. The President may call him in to find out what all the fuss is about. And at no time can he clearly identify the forces arrayed against him. His opponents are masters of the circuitous route.

Every President puts forward reorganization plans. So do most governors. But they can never afford to tell the public in all candor what vested interests are blocking the reorganization and why. So they never gain the support that public indignation would provide. Citizen groups should call for reorganization of executive agencies, should publicly identify the hidden alliances sabotaging reorganization, and should rally public support for government that works.

THE CONCENTRATION OF ECONOMIC POWER

With every year that passes, power in the business world becomes increasingly concentrated. Over two-thirds of all privately owned corporate stock is now in the hands of 2 percent of American families. In 1968 the 100 largest firms had a greater share of manufacturing assets than the 200 largest had in 1950, and as great as the 1,000 largest had in 1941. In the years from 1948 to 1968 the 200 largest firms bought up 3,900 other companies. Some 4,550 firms disappeared through a merger in 1969 alone. In 1945, there were about a thousand privately owned utility systems; in 1970, there were only 300. General Motors has an annual revenue

greater than that of any foreign government except the United Kingdom and the USSR.

Former Attorney General John Mitchell said, "In 1948, the nation's 200 largest industrial corporations controlled 48 percent of manufacturing assets. Today they control 58 percent, while the top 500 firms control 75 percent of these assets. The danger that this superconcentration poses to our economic, political, and social structure cannot be overestimated. Concentration of this magnitude is likely to eliminate existing and future competition. It increases the possibility for reciprocity and other forms of unfair buyer-seller coverage. It creates nationwide marketing managerial and financial structures whose enormous physical and psychological resources pose substantial barriers to small firms . . ." *

Back of the huge firms lies a perhaps greater power, the power of the institutional investors—mutual funds, pension funds, insurance companies, and banks. In 1969, for the first time, institutional investors traded more shares than did individuals.

The growing concentration of economic power in banks deserves special attention, and not only because, unlike most other institutional investors, banks have a lively interest in control of the companies in which they invest. The power of banks is greatly extended by their capacity to vote the portfolios of their trust ac-

---

* It says something about corporate political influence that the man who expressed those views appeared to be somewhat less than a rigorous guardian of the antitrust laws when the corporations involved had close ties with the administration. Serious questions were raised during Mitchell's tenure as attorney general when ITT, which had given or promised $400,000 to underwrite the Republican National Convention was allowed to merge with Hartford Fire Insurance; and when Warner–Lambert (whose chairman, Elmer Bobst, was one of Nixon's top political contributors in 1968) was allowed to merge with Parke, Davis.

67

counts. It is common practice for bank officers to sit on the board of companies in which they have invested heavily.

In 1971, commercial banks held $607 billion, just less than 60 percent of the $1 trillion held by institutional investors. In the years between 1950 and 1965 there were 2,200 bank mergers. By 1965, 100 of the 14,000 existing banks controlled 50 percent of all deposits. Fourteen of the 100 controlled 25 percent.

The emergence of the one-bank holding company has spread the web of influence still further. The holding company was designed to get around laws that limit banks to the business of banking. The number of such holding companies has increased enormously in the past fifteen years. In 1970, a law to check their growth was passed, but the law doesn't call for the break-up of existing companies.

The potential for unhealthy control by banks was revealed in a suit brought by the Department of Justice in April 1970 against the Cleveland Trust Company. The suit charged that the bank held and voted the stock of four major tool manufacturers, has representatives on all four boards, and influenced company policies of all four.

But banks are only an example—the most disturbing example perhaps—of an unmistakable trend toward ever-increasing concentration of power and wealth. Mergers continue to gobble up medium-size companies. The rise of the conglomerates has been startling in its consequences. The ramifying power-networks of the giant firms reach into every aspect of our lives.

It would be nice if one could believe that such enormous power would be exercised in the public interest, but the record is not encouraging—not just in recent times but as far back as the record runs. When Alfred P. Sloan, Jr., refused to install safety glass in General

Motors automobiles because it would narrow the profit margin, he said, "You can say, perhaps, that I am selfish, but business is selfish. We are not a charitable institution . . ."

The unbridled concentration of economic power leads to ever larger and more complex organizations. Everything we know about the corporate giants indicates that they do not increase efficiency beyond a certain point, and they foster monopolistic practices which are ultimately very costly to the consumer. (Senator Philip Hart says that because of such practices, "easily 30 percent of all consumer spending is wasted.")

But the gravest danger in the concentration of economic power is the increased capacity to influence the public process through the power of money. As that capacity increases, the forms and ceremonies of democracy become a mockery.

We need a large-scale and intensive study of the rise of the conglomerates, with special attention to their impact on the industries involved and upon individual firms taken over (in terms of management, morale, productivity, and so on). In the meantime existing antitrust legislation should be more vigorously enforced, and measures should be taken to curb the political influence of corporate giants (through campaign-spending controls, lobbying disclosure and conflict of interest statutes).

TAX REFORM

Latter-day populists use the phrase "redistribute the wealth" as a battle cry. There is no record of any multimillionaire losing sleep over the phrase, but it scares the wits out of the middle-income citizen who has just made the final payment on his house. Both he (who fears it) and the populists who seek it talk as though "the redistribution of wealth" is something that is not now happening but might be made to happen. Actually it is going on all the time and its chief instrument is the tax system. When redistribution benefits the poor it does so under charity-soaked words such as "welfare." When it benefits the rich it does so under businesslike labels such as "provision of economic incentives." Whichever direction the money moves it is coin of the realm and not rejected by the recipient.

A seventeenth-century Englishman said, "Give me the making of the songs of a nation, and I care not who makes its laws." Many an American businessman, possessing the same delicate perception of differing roles, might say "Give me the making of the nation's tax laws, and I care not who governs." One might think that a process so central to economic justice as the shaping of the tax laws would be the subject of intense public scrutiny. But it is not. It is surrounded by a secrecy that makes it impossible to hold one's elected representatives accountable. And behind the curtain of secrecy, some curious things happen.

In 1970, 112 individuals with annual incomes of more than $200,000 were legally able to avoid paying any federal income taxes. Three of the 112 reported incomes of more than one million. That's the kind of information that has convinced a lot of ordinary hard-working taxpaying Americans that they're playing in a game where someone has stacked the deck.

Joseph Pechman, one of the leading tax authorities in the country, has said that income tax rates could be lowered one-third with no resulting reduction in the amount of money raised if all income were subject to tax and the personal deductions were pruned to the essential items.

Depletion allowances, the capital gains tax, the many

avenues of escape from the estate tax, the abuse of farm tax losses, accelerated depreciation, and innumerable other devices enable the high-income taxpayer to bring his tax rate far below that of citizens in the middle- and lower income ranges.

Nobody likes to pay taxes. But if this nation is to solve its problems, the citizen is going to pay more, not less, in taxes. Faced with that painful reality, the citizen is going to demand that the tax system be equitable. It is not equitable today.

Tax reform must be high on the priority list of those who would restore the citizen's lost confidence in government. But there will be no tax reform without congressional reform. In the long run an equitable tax system will not come about until we impose the requirements of responsiveness and accountability on the House Ways and Means Committee and the Senate Finance Committee.

The secrecy with which the revenue committees operate must be ended. The closed rule, which prohibits any amendments to a tax bill coming out of the Ways and Means Committee, must be abolished.

And there is a third requirement. Conference committees on revenue legislation must reflect the majority views in both Senate and House. After the House and the Senate has each voted its version of a tax bill, a "conference committee," consisting of members from the House Ways and Means Committee and the Senate Finance Committee, is appointed to resolve differences between House and Senate versions. The iron rule of seniority has in the past determined who gets named to the conference committee, and this has had the effect of stacking the cards against tax reform proposals voted by the Senate. In recent years, conference committees on tax bills have invariably failed to include a majority of senators who voted for major tax reform amendments.

CHAPTER FIVE

Citizen Action

THE MORE one examines the web of influence woven by special interests and the accommodation of politicians to that influence, the less one anticipates changes from within the political system itself. It must come from citizens. They will never produce totally sanitary politics; but they can and must regain command of their own instruments of self-government.

Institutions don't overhaul themselves. They find it painful. When an institution is in need of renewal, someone must shake it up. In the case of political institutions, the shakeup must come from concerned citizens determined to create responsive government, determined to bring the parties to life, determined to cut through organizational dry rot and revitalize aging institutions.

THE EMERGENCE OF CITIZEN ACTION

It is no accident that Common Cause was launched in 1970. The time was ripe. Future historians may remember the 1970s as the decade when citizen action emerged as a revitalizing force in American society. If so, they will not report it as a new thing but as a familiar ingredient in American life that matured and came into its own.

They will note that, in the decades preceding the emergence, the American people had ignored their duties as citizens. They had allowed their instruments of self-government to fall into disrepair. They had allowed themselves to be smothered by large-scale organization and technology and all the glittering promises of modernity. They had almost forgotten the national attribute described 130 years earlier in the familiar passage from de Tocqueville.

> These Americans are the most peculiar people in the world . . . in a local community in their country a citizen may conceive of some need which is not being met. What does he do? He goes across the street and discusses it with his neighbor.
>
> Then what happens? A committee comes into existence . . . All of this is done without reference to any bureaucrat. All of this is done by private citizens on their own initiative.

The world was simpler then. As our society grew vast and complex, we became less and less sure of our capacity to act on our own initiative as citizens. Certainly, Americans in the mid-twentieth century manifested little of the confident approach to their common problems that de Tocqueville observed.

Then in the 1960s a feeling for citizen action reappeared with extraordinary vigor. It was foreshadowed in the 1950s in the civil rights movement. In the 1960s the students raised the cry of "participatory democracy." Among the poor the phrase was "community action." The peace movement, the conservation movement, the family planning movement emerged as potent elements in our national life.

Much of this activity was diffuse, erratic, and poorly organized. But little by little citizen action began to develop a more professional cutting edge. Ralph Nader demonstrated what could be accomplished by a tough-minded professional approach. The civil rights movement proved that it could move history-making legislation through Congress against immensely powerful and entrenched opponents. And young civil rights lawyers were among the first to explore the full possibilities of what is now called public interest law.

The new aggressiveness and determination behind citizen action was clearly reflected in the public fight to deny Senate confirmation to Judge G. Harrold Carswell, President Nixon's nominee for the Supreme Court. When the nomination was submitted in January 1970, virtually everyone assumed that it would be accepted. The Senate had just rejected the nomination of Clement Haynsworth, and few senators wanted to enter into a second pitched battle against the massive combined strength of the administration, the Republican right wing, and the Southern bloc. But the handful of senators who were willing to oppose the nomination turned out to have a potent resource: the willing hands of many citizens. Civil rights groups led the battle. Members of the legal profession were slower to join in, but were enormously effective when they did so. Some of the most impressive contributions were those from a group of Columbia University law students whose study of Judge Carswell's published decisions revealed that he had been reversed by higher courts nearly 60 percent of the time, a third more frequently than the average of his fellow judges. The labor movement, the academic world, and other articulate segments of the electorate joined in. The firm votes against the nomination increased, first with agonizing slowness and then more rapidly. And the nomination was defeated.

Even more dramatic was the defeat of the supersonic transport (SST) in December 1970 and again in March 1971. Lined up in favor of the SST were the administration, the aviation industry, most conservatives, and most businessmen—in other words, all of the "clout" that those who call themselves political realists so reverently celebrate. Arrayed against the SST was an unlikely and not very well organized coalition of citizen groups, chiefly environmentalists. A tough-minded Washingtonian can die laughing at the futility of action by earnest and well-intentioned citizens. But by March of 1971, no proponent of the SST was laughing. The SST was dead. The money-heavy lobby for the SST that operated out of downtown Washington offices was left with its pamphlets down. The citizens had won.

Such nationally publicized episodes do not capture one of the chief attributes of the new wave of citizen action, viz., that similar action is also taking place in thousands of communities and neighborhoods as citizens speak out on local issues.

What we are seeing is the beginnings of a powerful movement to call the great institutions of our society to account. The ombudsman concept is being tried in various places. Young lawyers are using litigation in ingenious ways to call private and public agencies to account. Consumerism, which is so far largely a middle-class phenomenon, is essentially the same kind of effort. All of the groping efforts at neighborhood organization are part of the same phenomenon.

The new politics and the politics of protest offer some innovative ways in which citizens can needle the great institutions of our society and demand an accounting of them. But as the movement continues, the American citizen is going to make a startling discovery. He is going to find that most of the new techniques for citizen action pale to insignificance before the enormous unused potential of the instruments of self-government that the citizen has allowed to grow rusty and out of repair. Until he turns again to those instruments, scrapes away the rust, repairs them, and resharpens them, perhaps even redesigns them, he will not regain command of his society.

THE HISTORY OF CITIZENS' MOVEMENTS

We mustn't be sentimental about what "the people" can accomplish. The resistance to change that any institution exhibits is not simply the mindless working of habit and custom. Those who enjoy power and privilege in a society preserve that power and privilege by weaving a tough protective web of custom, rules, processes, and institutional structure. Can we really expect that any citizens' movement will be strong enough and determined enough to cut through that web?

It is a crucial question, and most experienced observers would probably answer "No." There is widespread skepticism as to the impact of popular movements. But the historical record does not bear out the skepticism.

The Populist Movement in the nineteenth century altered both of the major parties before it ran out of steam. Citizens' movements led to the abolition of child labor and to the vote for women. A popular movement foisted Prohibition on the nation and a second popular movement repealed it. Relatively small groups of crusading citizens launched the labor movement, the civil rights movement, the peace movement, the conservation movement, the family planning movement. All of these welled up from the ranks of the people. None was launched by government action. Nor could they have been. But they made the government respond.

76

Before 1969, the organized conservation movement consisted of no more than two or three hundred thousand citizens. But they won allies among editors, among writers, among congressmen, among opinion-makers—and they pushed the environmental issue to the top of the national agenda. How long would we have had to wait for such action to emerge from the bureaucracy? Forever would be a fair estimate.

Only on the rarest occasions are significant new directions in public policy initiated by the legislature, or by the bureaucracy, or by the parties. They are initiated by the people—not "The People" taken collectively, but by vigorous and forward-looking elements within the body politic. Or they are initiated by the special interests.

THE ROLE OF CITIZEN ACTION

Skeptics contrast the supposed impracticality of citizens' movements with the "hard realities of politics." But popular movements have proven themselves to be the hardest of realities. They have had a profound impact on the political process. The surge of citizen opinion on a given subject is always underestimated at first by politicians. But if it continues, they take it into account. Citizen opinion, massively expressed, is a form of power; and politicians are power brokers.

When we see the strength of these movements, when we see that they have often forced great issues to the attention of the bureaucracy, we begin to sense a creative force in American life that has not been fully appreciated.

In our society any group of citizens can identify a problem, offer a solution, and attempt to persuade the rest of the nation of their rightness. They nominate themselves. If the early feminists or civil rights leaders or conservationists had waited for a referendum to anoint them as the legitimate leaders of a movement, they'd still be waiting. But just as a free society gives them full rein to nominate themselves, so it reserves the right to ignore them (and thus seal their doom).

Crusading citizens' groups may not always be wise, as witness the Prohibitionists. Or they may be wise but unsuccessful in persuading their fellow citizens. For every citizens' group that changes the course of history, there are thousands, perhaps hundreds of thousands, that never create a ripple. Even of those that do make a ripple, many have a short life. They trail off into ineffectual pamphleteering, or live on as museum pieces dusted faithfully by aging followers. Or they just disappear.

The people are the soil. The movements are seeds. Some never germinate. Some die early. A few prosper and grow strong. The whole process provides the society with a superb source of new growth. It provides ample opportunity for the testing of ideas—good ideas, ordinary ideas, dismal ideas. Only the ideas with vitality survive the testing. And only the ones with a powerful popular impact will affect history. *The great virtue of a free people is to be that fertile seedbed, not, as some have supposed, to be always right or enlightened but to be the soil from which enlightenment can spring.*

The surging creative quality of popular movements gains its real significance in contrast to the limited creativity of institutions, or to put it more harshly, the tendency of *all* institutions to decay, to rigidify, and to stifle new ideas. It is not a peculiar weakness of our own society. It has been true of all human institutions since the beginning.

The hardened professionals of this world look with condescension on the undisciplined enthusiasm of citizens' movements. But the one thing that is worse than undisciplined ardor is no ardor at all. That is one of the reasons why the individual citizen can be creative when institutions are not. How often does one see an ardent institution? The exhilaration of the crusade resides in the individual breast. The institution is by nature prudent, rational, cool, systematic, and self-preserving. It shrinks from challenge and risk. It is unbloody but bowed.

Enthusiasm is perhaps too limited a word to denote what I am talking about. The world will be changed, if it is changed at all, by men and women of exceptional vitality—vitality that has not been sapped by despair or physical deprivation, vitality that has not been drained away by the enervating climate of bureaucracy, vitality that has been released by anger or indignation.

The Spanish have a saying, "In Spain everything decays but the race." It is a universal condition. Nations decay; only the citizen, critical and loving, can bring them back to life. Institutions are weighted with the past; the individual is on the side of vitality and the future.

IS PUBLIC INTEREST LOBBYING LEGITIMATE?

Common Cause has described itself as "a citizens' lobby." But the idea of a citizens' lobby raises questions. One is whether the very concept of a lobby—even a lobby run by well-intentioned citizens—isn't somehow reprehensible. One distinguished American said to the founders of Common Cause: "*All* lobbies should be abolished by law. In a democracy we should elect the best possible people and then expect them to follow their own best judgment without pressure from *any* group—even a well-motivated one."

What he failed to understand is that the right of any group, well-motivated or not, to try to influence government decisions is constitutionally protected in the "right to petition" clause of the First Amendment. It cannot be abolished.

From the beginning of the Republic, special-interest groups and more broadly based citizen movements have sought to influence government. Lobbying activities are carried out not only by commercial interests but by groups representing labor unions, universities, the professions, religious groups, and many others.

All experts on government accept lobbying as a legitimate part of the political process. The problem is not that it exists but that it is almost always carried on in behalf of special interests, almost never in behalf of the public interest. Everybody's organized but the people.

INTEREST GROUP PLURALISM

There are those who recognize the legitimacy of lobbying but say it should be left to the special interests because no group of citizens, however high-minded, can take it upon themselves to say what is in the public interest. This view reflects a lingering belief in so-called interest-group pluralism. According to that doctrine, each special group pursues its own selfish concerns, but taken all together they somehow balance one another out and the public interest is served. Given the obvious dominance of special interests in our national life, that is an enormously comforting doctrine.

The only trouble is that it isn't true. Very often the

public interest is not served. All the special interests clashing in the urban setting have not somehow balanced out to produce wise and far-seeing urban solutions. The public interest in clean air and water has not been served by the clash of special interests in the environmental field.

Interest-group pluralism has accounted for a good deal of our dynamism as a nation, but it has clear limita tions. Let us preserve it, let us expect that it will serve us in important ways, but let us not imagine that it will do all the things that need to be done. Too often the public interest and the interests of the ordinary individual fall between the stools of the special-interest groups. We need the special-interest groups, but we also need a strong voice for the public interest. If the system were working perfectly, our instruments of self-government would be that strong voice. When they fail to function as such, in our free society, groups of citizens make themselves heard directly. It's a tradition as old as the nation.

THE CONCEPT OF THE PUBLIC INTEREST

Obviously, no sensible person approaches the idea of the public interest without caution. It is a tricky concept. The farmer wants higher prices for his produce and the factory worker wants cheap food. Which is in the public interest? The citizen as conservationist fights to prevent location of a new power plant in his vicinity, while the citizen as homeowner seeks more and more electric power for his appliances. Which is in the public interest?

But such perplexities simply confirm that social policy is difficult to formulate. If it were impossible for citizens to agree on *anything* that could be defined as the public interest—if there were no common ground of any sort—then there could be no Constitution, no criminal code, and no way of living together peaceably from day to day.

No citizens' movement should assume that it has some divinely inspired grasp of what is "in the public interest." It must have the courage of its convictions, but it must present those convictions in the public forum where all other groups can debate their validity. Everything it does it must do openly. And though it is a petitioner (and therefore often an adversary) in relation to the government, it must ultimately respect the public process. That is why a citizens' movement must be interested in the structure and process of government. It should not wish to substitute itself for political and governmental institutions as the *vox populi*. *It should want the instruments of free self-government to work. It should want the freely elected representatives of the people to represent them wisely and well.*

No particular group should identify itself as *the* citizens' lobby. Common Cause is *a* citizens' lobby taking its place among many other citizens' groups that are working in what they conceive to be the public interest.

It is a mistake to view citizen action as outside politics. It is an integral part of the political process. I have heard observers describe Common Cause as being "above politics." It is *not* above politics. It is merely nonpartisan.

THE CONSTRAINTS ON ELECTIVE OFFICIALS

But can a citizens' lobby be effective? The deepest skepticism on that point comes from those who believe that the election of good men and women to public office is the beginning and end of political wisdom. "If you want to change things," they say, "elect men and women who will bring about the desired changes."

The reality is considerably less simple. Often even "good" candidates begin long before election to accommodate themselves to the very forces in American life that they would have to oppose if they were to accomplish significant change. Sometimes they cannot even be nominated unless they put themselves under obligation to a corrupt political machine. Often they accept campaign gifts from powerful corporate, union, or professional groups whose interests they will later be required to weigh against the public interest. Too often, when they enter office they find themselves deeply compromised by those pre-election accommodations.

And even if they have been wise enough not to make such accommodations, they discover, upon being elected, that they are trapped in political and governmental machinery that cannot be made to work.

I think we would all agree that if we could, in any given election year, increase by 15 or 20 percent the number of good people in public office, it would be a remarkable feat—a stunning feat. Yet, I am convinced that if we were to accomplish that stunning feat it would make very little difference. Very few of the things that are really wrong with this country would be altered.

Powerful as he may seem, a President's options are limited—limited by the accommodations he made in order to get elected, limited by his desire to be re-elected (or to keep his party in power), limited by the structure and constraints of governmental institutions.

Even if Presidents were as powerful as some citizens think they are, there is no evidence that the American people will consistently—or even frequently—elect Presidents with the greatness and wisdom to initiate profound and far-reaching social changes. I have asked many experienced observers, "How often can we expect to have in the White House a man who has the intellect, character, charisma, stamina, and courage to provide truly inspired Presidential leadership?" The pessimists say once or twice in a century. The most optimistic say once in a quarter century. Clearly we cannot organize our society in such a way that we are dependent on inspired Presidential leadership, because most of the time it won't be there.

We must build creative strength in other parts of the system. And in fact that's the kind of system it was intended to be. It was never intended that we should seek a Big Daddy and lean on him. We shall save ourselves—or we won't be saved.

It is immensely important that we elect a President of superior qualifications. But we cannot put sole reliance on him nor on any of our other elected officials to bring about the deep changes in our institutions that are essential. Without an active, concerned constituency they are helpless.

CHAPTER SIX

Effectiveness in Citizen Action

THE MOST important thing the reader should know about citizen action is that it can work. It has worked. It is working.

The next most important thing to know is that enthusiasm isn't enough. If citizen action is to be successful it requires careful preparation, effective organization, and stamina. Lots and lots of stamina. As Arthur Vanderbilt said of court reform, it is no sport for the shortwinded. And purity of motive is no substitute for well-conceived, well-executed, sustained action.

There has been more enthusiasm than realism about citizen action, and critics are justified in asking hard questions about any group such as Common Cause. How does it expect to bring about changes? How will it cope with the powerful vested interests that it will confront? Where will it acquire the clout that lobbies are supposed to have?

We are still far from having all the answers. But we have a few.

SUSTAINED ACTION

Perhaps the first rule is that an effective instrument of citizen action must be a full-time, continued "presence" on the scene. One of the deepest failings of citizen action is the here-today-gone-tomorrow campaign, the unpredictable waxing and waning of enthusiasm. In matters of significant social action, the forces opposing change are powerful and deeply rooted. They have little respect for adversaries who lack staying power.

An example of the need for sustained effort is the experience with campaign-spending control legislation in 1970–1971. After the elections of 1970, the scandalous laxity of our campaign-financing laws became a live public issue. It was on the front pages and the editorial pages. It was in the cartoons. There were powerful stories by the ablest investigative reporters.

That was in December 1970 and January 1971. But it takes time to draft legislation, to hold hearings, to bring significant legislative proposals to a vote. Eight months elapsed before legislation was moving toward a crucial test. And by that time the public was bored with the subject. Editors shunted stories to the back pages. And once again the public interest was in danger of being butchered. Fortunately, both editorial and public interest revived and a law was passed in early 1972.

FOCUSED ACTION

An equally important rule of citizen action is to select a limited number of clearly defined targets and hit them hard. Among the most familiar weaknesses of citizen action are the diffusion of energy and resources over too many targets, the brave but trivial effort, and the failure to tackle concrete, tangible, achievable goals. Citizen action scattered enthusiastically in all directions changes nothing. The accomplishment of significant change requires clear-cut targets and a massing of energy and resources.

In Common Cause we guard against aimless dissipation of energy by a simple operating philosophy: with rare exceptions, we do nothing but fight specific battles —legal or legislative. We enter each battle seeking a specific outcome. And we stay with it until we win or lose.

We do not engage in educational campaigns for their own sake, nor research for its own sake (though we use the research of others). Nor do we make pronouncements or engage in debate on any issue unless we intend to fight that issue through to a conclusion.

That operating philosophy has forced us to focus our energies and resources on specific targets. It has spared us the vague and intangible efforts to "do good" that absorb so much of the energies of well-intentioned organizations. Sometimes we win, sometimes we lose, but it is never intangible.

The concrete nature of the goal is crucial. Let me illustrate the point. From the beginning of Common Cause, we have been deeply concerned with advancing the principle of *accountability* in government, but the goal could not be pursued in terms of abstractions. Nor could we pursue it on a thousand fronts. We chose a specific battleground, the seniority system.

To take another example, we believe that citizens should have access to their political institutions and that those institutions should be responsive. We had to translate those abstractions into a concrete issue on which we could do battle, and the issue we chose was campaign spending. Uncontrolled campaign financing makes for political institutions that are accessible and responsive to money rather than to people.

A PROFESSIONAL CUTTING EDGE

Another weakness of the citizen in political action is unwillingness to acquire a grasp of the processes of government. Too often he can't be bothered with the grimy machinery by which the public business gets done. He is content to "leave that to the technicians." But people who control the course of events leave nothing to the technicians. Often they *are* the technicians.

It isn't in politics only that high-minded citizens shy away from the nuts and bolts of action. In every other field of practical action they show the same distaste for the unglamorous details by which victories are won or lost. And it is always disastrous. Significant social change is accomplished by men and women with a vision in their heads and a monkey wrench in their hands. Ideals without a program are fantasy. And a program without organization is a hoax.

Part of the reason for these failures of the high-minded citizen is self-indulgence. He feels so noble just "fighting the good fight" that he finds rewards even in defeat. And he often seems to believe—if only unconsciously—that high-mindedness is a substitute for professional skill in doing battle. No wonder he loses so often.

PUBLIC INFORMATION

Effective communication is the most powerful single weapon of the public interest lobby.

The special interest lobby usually works behind closed doors. It rarely reveals (or wants to reveal) what goes on in the back room. In contrast, the public interest lobby wants to tell the whole story—what's at stake, who stands to gain or lose, who's making what deals. A long time ago, Frank Kent said one of the basic rules of politics is "Never handle a hot poker on the front porch." But that is just where the citizen wants to see the poker handled.

The light of day has a marvelously cleansing effect on politicians. H. L. Mencken said that "Conscience is the inner voice that warns us somebody may be looking." Nowhere is it more true than in public life. Possibly the greatest achievement of conservationists in the past half-dozen years is that they have persuaded literally hundreds of federal, state, and local agencies concerned with the environment that "somebody may be looking."

The citizen's lobby must seek out and translate into clear language the information that the public needs to have on any given issue. The story must be told in the mass media. Citizens must write to their local newspapers about it, discuss it in their church or union groups, talk to their friends about it. The issue must be dramatized. If the public is apathetic, it must be aroused. If there is already public indignation, it must be channeled.

ALLIANCES

Another elementary rule for the citizens' group is to form alliances with other citizen organizations. Unlike the institutional side of our national life, which has become increasingly monolithic, citizen action expresses itself through innumerable channels. New citi-

89

zens' groups sprout like blades of grass after a spring rain. And they are of little value in fighting major battles of social change unless those with common objectives work together.

It isn't easily accomplished. Organizational vanity creeps into the noblest organizations. Each group has its own version of what is important, what the solutions are, and what constitutes an unacceptable compromise.

The most effective alliances occur when groups of similar purpose set up *ad hoc* arrangements to work together on a specific battle. Longer-term alliances are virtually impossible. They invite the creation of "coordinating mechanisms" and other exercises in futility. The *ad hoc* alliance may consist of nothing more than an agreement among representatives of various groups to meet weekly (or daily) as a legislative fight approaches. The minimum purpose is to share information. But a division of labor usually emerges as each group sees that it can serve the common purpose in some specially effective way.

The potential force of such collaboration may be seen when one reflects on the size of some groups involved. It is possible, given an appropriate issue, to gather into one room on a week's notice a dozen people from organizations representing tens of millions of Americans.

A citizens' movement should also make the most of allies within the institution it is trying to affect. There are many public officials, elective and appointive, who want very much to improve the institutions in which they find themselves, and welcome the helping hand of a citizens' movement. They can be invaluable allies and advisers. A citizens' movement makes a grave mistake if it imagines that it is so right—and so righteous—that a working public servant couldn't possibly contribute to its store of wisdom.

MEMBERSHIP AS CADRE

The citizens' group should treat its membership as a cadre, not a "bloc" in the electoral sense. The goal is not vast numbers but an *active* membership that multiplies its effectiveness by reaching out into the community. There are private-sector organizations that number their members in millions, yet have little influence because their membership is inert. Such organizations are usually long-established, complacent, and routine-ridden. The formula for organizational vitality in a citizens' group is a smaller number of genuinely active members.

And activity in members is directly related to form of organization. It is odd but true that many groups that profess an interest in action are not in fact organized for action. Some, though asserting an interest in action, are organized essentially for study and discussion. Others appear to be organized chiefly to educate. Still others have a mode of organization that serves primarily to keep the members busy with organizational housekeeping, ego-gratifying committee chores, internal politics, and the interminable passing of resolutions. Most citizens' organizations either talk themselves to death or bureaucratize themselves into a state of paralysis. It is a devil of a job to get action out of an organization that isn't designed for action.

THE MIDDLE

Something remains to be said about the target of the action. Significant change depends on reaching the middle range of opinion. It isn't easily done,

91

because perception of the need for significant change begins with a few individuals who are sufficiently far-sighted to comprehend the problems that lie ahead and to propose solutions. Such *avant-garde* individuals naturally hope that the truth they see will gain wider acceptance; but they would not have seen that truth in the first place had they not been more independent-minded than their fellows. And many of them, because of that very independence of mind, are rather contemptuous (consciously or not) of the more conformist middle range of opinion. They are rarely conscious of the dilemma this poses: for their truth to be widely accepted they must teach it to a segment of the populace of which they are contemptuous. Since contempt isn't a particularly winning attitude in a leader or teacher, they often antagonize potential converts.

A citizens' movement can't afford such self-indulgence. It must acknowledge—and not grudgingly—that the active participation of the middle is crucial to its success.

The task of educating citizens in the middle of the political spectrum to the grave choices ahead is bound to be supremely difficult. Such education must be carried on in a national climate that is seething with political movements, special interests, conflicting ideologies, slogans, battle cries, appeals to emotion, and deep-rooted prejudice. Some of the choices facing the citizen require a fairly deep understanding of what we face as a world; and anyone promoting that understanding must compete with opponents pursuing far shallower objectives, opponents who will not hesitate to play upon anxiety, hatred, fear, prejudice, and the desire for instant gain.

One favorable circumstance is that over the past generation the middle segment of the population has become more educated and accessible than ever before. This is a consequence not only of education in the formal sense but of the heightened awareness that comes from living in a communications-saturated world. The increased education and heightened awareness make it difficult for citizens to continue the old unthinking acceptance of party labels, interest-group politics, corrupt city machines, and venal politicians. Their minds have been opened to larger realities and possibilities.

But no group as politically, culturally, and economically heterogeneous as "the middle" moves of its own volition. It responds to an active ingredient within it, a leadership element, if you will.

Common Cause made the rather risky assumption that in matters bearing on the public interest, such an activist element could be identified and mobilized. And the assumption proved correct.

A CONSTITUENCY FOR THE PUBLIC INTEREST

Not only have we found "a constituency for the public interest," we have discovered that when they see an opportunity to act constructively they are capable of great enthusiasm and dedication.

Some critics, it is true, have still not accepted the idea. How, they ask, could we assemble "a constituency for the public interest" when most of our members are involved in their own special interests? Are they not businessmen, union members, minority leaders, doctors, and so on, who will fragment along the lines of their special interests when controversial issues arise?

We did not accept the assumption of the critics that everyone is a prisoner of his special interests. But prior to launching Common Cause we could not refute that assumption decisively. Now we can.

Every citizen has a stake in the public interest, and

some citizens have the good sense to understand that very clearly. Because some citizens understand it, there is already a constituency for the public interest. But it is an unassembled constituency. The individuals who make it up wear no labels, nor do they come from any one segment of society. But they exist. We have seen them in action.

Perhaps most physicians think primarily in terms of the vested interest of the medical profession. But there is a percentage (to avoid undue optimism, let's say a modest percentage) who see their profession as part of the larger social enterprise and who know that their special professional interest and the public interest are not wholly separable. They see that it is *to their own advantage* to serve both their profession and the society. They are a part of the unassembled constituency for the public interest. They are the kind of people who should belong to Common Cause.

Similarly, most businessmen may see the world through the special blinders of commercial vested interest. But a modest percentage see that it is a matter of elementary self-interest to work as well for the good of the larger community. They see that they cannot prosper for long if the community deteriorates.

In the same way, we have found in every other field—labor, the professions, the universities, and so on—people capable of seeing how much their own self-interest is caught up in the public interest. We are drawing our membership from the people in every field who understand those realities. One of the reasons it is crucially important to maintain an open society, without barriers of race or class or economic conditions, is so that those extraordinarily valuable men and women will have access to the channels of influence and decision.

Who are these people who have the wit to perceive and the courage to act in behalf of the public interest?

They are to be found in every social class and every segment of the society. They aren't necessarily the best-known people in their neighborhoods, rarely are they the most powerful. But they are natural builders of the political and moral order. Man has always created coherent societies in which to live. It is no accident that every human society has had —in no matter how primitive a form—a moral and political order. Man is an order-producing animal. As beavers build dams, man builds moral and political orders. He can't help it. It is in him to do so.

The strength of the impulse varies from one person to the next. In some it seems nonexistent. In others it is an impulse of overwhelming power. It can be observed among members of every race, every level, every cultural tradition.

It would be a lot easier to describe—and to dramatize —the constituency for the public interest if its members fitted some familiar stereotype or category. If only they all were liberals or all conservatives or all of one political party. Or if only they used familiar slogans or shared some easily identified ideology! But they don't. What they share is a concern for the public interest.

By no means all of those citizens who share a concern for the public interest share an interest in politics. Many have grown up scorning politics, and others who were once politically inclined have dropped out. They can't respect the party hacks. They can't stomach the old dogmas. They don't see how they can be effective politically. They see no party they want to associate themselves with.

A major task of Common Cause has been to persuade these citizens that they can and should be active politically. And the first goal of such political activity should be to open up the public process to all the people. It is a mistake to suppose that the problems facing the nation can be solved by any one group of citizens, no matter how high-minded. Any group that makes that mistake will end up imagining itself a new elite—and that would be a sad end for a people's movement. No one can know what segment of the populace will—if given a voice—play a creative role in bringing new issues to light or forcing us to face up to crucial problems of our future. The doors must remain open for all elements within the society to have their say. The instruments of self-government through which all elements can have their say already exist. The first goal of citizens concerned for the public interest is to make those instruments responsive.

Those citizens who care about the public interest must know that their contributions to society are needed and welcome. We are not dealing here with an aristocracy possessing an aristocratic consciousness of role. Nor with a managerial or military caste in which the members are marked by rank, income, or title. The people I'm talking about are scattered among the population—a housewife here, a union member there, a business entrepreneur, a salesman.

They need encouragement. And they need organization. Common Cause can and will supply both. But Common Cause will not be the only organization serving the citizen who is concerned for the public interest —nor should it be. There will be various conceptions of the public interest and how it may best be served, and there is room for various organizations.

One of the problems plaguing such citizens at the moment is that they are not happy with the leadership they see in the public arena. This, I believe, is a problem that can solve itself. When the new constituency emerges as a political force it will call forth leaders worthy of it —not one but many.

CHAPTER SEVEN

First Steps in a Long Journey

THE STORM warnings are out. Our problem is to understand them. In every case of a civilization that has died, there were countless signals of the disaster to come. But the leaders were deaf.

FORKS IN THE ROAD AHEAD

In our own case, what do the storm warnings portend? What are they trying to say to us?

I think they are trying to tell us that an era is ending and another era is about to begin. Something new is struggling to be born. We can't say what it will be, but we can say with certainty what some of the forks in the road ahead will be.

We will move toward some system of arms control, strengthening of the United Nations and world rule of law—*or we will see crippling arms competition, multiple small wars, and growing danger of the final war.*

We will create a reasonably stable social and political order based on institutions responsive and accountable to free citizens, institutions that seek liberty and justice for all, institutions in which the worth of the individual is not based on race, sex, money, or status—*or we will see the emergence of a coercive order.* (Disorder is not an option.)

We will re-establish some measure of harmony with our natural environment through pollution control and population control—*or we will see irreversible destruction of our planetary environment at the same time that we are burdening it with more human beings than it can support.*

We will create a society in which technology and large-scale organizations are so designed and developed as to serve human needs—*or technology and large-scale organization will become, irrevocably, our master and not our servant.*

We will preserve a society in which the media are free and internal communication untrammeled—*or we will fall victim to the limitless possibilities for manipulation of information inherent in modern social organization.*

Those are only a few of the more fateful choices. The phrase "fork in the road" is not quite suitable because it suggests a single point in time at which a decision is made. On any of the items listed, the outcome will be the cumulative result of many decisions made over time. Also, the phrase "fork in the road" suggests more freedom of choice on our part than is actually the case. There are powerful historical forces at work, and our contemporary decisions will only partially determine the outcome. But to have only a partially decisive role has always been the human condition. All the more reason to play that role to the hilt.

WHY INSTITUTIONS AND SOCIETIES GROW OLD

Institutions and societies lose their adaptability for three basic reasons. First, the dominant groups weave an impenetrable web of procedure, law, and social structure to preserve their power and in doing so cut themselves off from the sources of rejuvenation: uncomfortable challenges and dissent. Second, the forces of inertia, habit, and custom elevate existing procedures to inviolable traditions: meeting current challenges becomes less important than preserving familiar arrangements. Third, a society loses the motivation, conviction, confidence, and morale that characterized it in its days of vitality. It no longer believes in anything, least of all in itself. The vision fades. The idea fails.

We have discussed ways of coping with the first two factors. It is time to talk about the third. It is clear that we must rebuild confidence and conviction concerning the aims and the future of our society. Unless the society can recapture a belief in its values and in the possibility of making those values live in action, its days are numbered. The result cannot be achieved by distinguished commissions that formulate goals for the nation. It cannot be done by rhetoric. It can be done only by the citizens themselves. They must act in behalf of their values, and they must experience some success in that action. Citizens are the resource—the only resource—that will heal this nation and set it on a path to greatness.

WHAT DO WE WANT?

But where do we want the nation to be headed?

One means of answering that question would be to remind ourselves of how the American people see their needs. There have been many studies of the concerns and aspirations of the people, and they sketch a fairly consistent portrait.

It is not a bizarre portrait. Most Americans are moved most of the time by a sensible self-interest.

First, citizens are concerned with simple, understandable needs: their health, good schools for their children, their jobs, their housing, and whether they will have enough money to pay the bills. It follows that they worry about skyrocketing rents, increases in unemployment, the difficulty of getting adequate health care, and all the things that affect their real income, particularly inflation.

Beyond immediate human needs, they want justice, equal opportunity, respect, and a sense of dignity as individuals. As long as these rights are not denied, citizens give them little thought. But if the rights are denied, the citizen's reaction is intense. Passive submission to injustice was once common. It is becoming less so every day. And basic rights *are* being denied many of our people today. Racial injustice is a continuing reality. Women do not have equal opportunity. Too many of our aged citizens are subjected to profound indignities. Too many children experience early deprivation from which they never recover.

In a larger context, citizens want reassurance concerning the stability of their world and a measure of hope for the years ahead. They would like to have some confidence in the ability of their society to solve its problems. They would like to believe the future will open out for themselves and their children. They worry about present and future threats to stablity and the enhancement of life—threats such as war, national disunity, crime, drugs, pollution, urban chaos, and social disintegration.

A VIEW OF THE FUTURE

Recognition that citizens want "a measure of hope for the future" forces us to reflect on a sharp change in our attitudes toward what lies ahead.

Americans once believed in Progress. They believed that they were an exceptionally virtuous citizenry. They believed that they inhabited the Best Country on Earth. And they were confident that the path leading to the future was onward and upward.

True, much of their faith was naïve. It involved a willingness to avert one's eyes from the poverty and injustice that existed then as much as now. It involved a childlike affirmation of our own way as against the way of all other nations. It was complacent and hypocritical. But on balance it was no more distorted than our present preoccupation with everything morbid in our national life, our sour refusal to be proud of our strengths and virtues.

The worst of our problem is not that the old vision is fading. Old visions are always fading. The question is whether we have lost the capacity to generate a new vision—or the capacity to tolerate visions. If so, we're in trouble.

I don't think we have lost that capacity. But we have

some preparatory work to do before a new vision can take hold. Since talk of "visions" is unnerving to the pragmatic modern mind, let me speak explicitly about that preparatory work.

If we are to regain anything approaching a confident view of our own future, we shall have to begin by proving to ourselves in tangible ways that we can be honest about our problems, that we have the guts to tackle them, and that we can solve *some* of them.

One cannot stress too strongly the importance of beginning with a concrete attack on concrete problems. The greatest barrier to a new vision is the awareness of how hypocritically we enshrined the old one. We enshrined it and defaced the shrine with our lies, our greed, our self-deception. In fact, we have been so hypocritical that several generations of intellectuals have developed a lively tradition of vision-debunking, and they may be incapable of the tough new assignment of vision-creating. We may have to turn the latter task over to younger and less-soured spirits.

But whoever creates the new vision will have to propose a means of achieving it. And it will grow strong only as we prove in action our commitment to it. After the citizen has decided where he wants the journey to take him, he still needs to know how to take the first step. That is why Common Cause, at this stage of its history, is concentrating on tangible, specific battles. As we discover that we can win specific battles, we will regain our sense of the future. We will build our shared vision out of a command of practicalities—jobs, health, housing, and workable political institutions. It is the only way to create a moral framework for a skeptical generation. We must create political, economic, and social institutions that make possible a realization of moral values—in other words, institution-building with a moral purpose. There's no point in talking of the dignity of the individual if we tolerate institutions that diminish and demean him.

A durable self-confidence doesn't demand instant victories, doesn't expect the ideal to translate itself into flawless reality, and doesn't rule out frequent defeats. It does demand concrete tangible signs of movement.

It is hardly surprising that among those who see most clearly the need for change, there are many who have a powerful impulse to reject *all* of the past. The new vision, they seem to be saying, must have no traces of the old. But, as Mr. Justice Holmes pointed out, "Historical continuity is not a duty, only a necessity." Our efforts are only the latest chapter in man's long history of moral and ethical striving. We cannot be so arrogant as to suppose otherwise.

Of course, there are those who believe that every trace of a moral tradition has long since been betrayed to the point of extinction. It has been betrayed, no doubt, and if betraying it could have destroyed it, it would have vanished very early in human history. But there is something stubborn about the moral strivings of our species. The striving survives betrayal. Or to put it more accurately, the effort to construct a moral order renews itself in each generation.

A FRAMEWORK OF VALUES

But what are the values we must build into our institutions? A good many Americans have begun to see the ingredients of a society that they could respect. In short, a great many of us now know what we want.

We want a society in which no one oppresses or exploits another and no one is excluded; in which "liberty and justice for all" are not just words in the Pledge of Allegiance; in which individuals are not coerced, victimized, or manipulated by institutions they can't understand and don't respect.

We want a society dedicated to the pursuit of peace; a society in which there is harmony between man and his natural environment; a society in which technology is the servant of human values.

We want a society in which a sense of community is still alive and a sense of identity is possible; in which individuality is not smothered by large-scale organization; in which every individual is needed and every person has the opportunity to serve.

We want a society in which political and governmental institutions are responsive and accountable, and each citizen has equal access to them; in which every citizen can have his say; in which participation is real and consequential—all this to the end that the individual may recover his capacity to act, to act for himself and in behalf of his community, with confidence and good spirit.

We want a society in which the individual can preserve, find, or create a moral framework that gives meaning, continuity, and dignity to his life and to our joint endeavors. We want a society in which the value placed on the dignity and worth of the individual is translated into decent housing, decent jobs, excellent schools, and adequate health care.

THE INDIVIDUAL AND SOCIETY

At the root of many, perhaps most, of the problems facing our social order today is the shattered relationship between the individual and the society. The attributes of our society that are responsible for the shattered relationship are familiar to all.

- —large-scale organization: monolithic, hierarchical, abstract, rational, programmed, artificial, tending to squeeze out pluralism, tending toward the beehive model.
- —the existence of techniques for dealing with large masses of the people, tending always toward the tyranny of the formula, toward the "processing" of human beings.
- —the tendency of rapidly evolving technology to over-ride individual human goals.
- —emphasis on the success ethic, on materialism, on commercialism.

It is easy to talk of villains who deliberately led us into those traps, but the truth is that most Americans acquiesced cheerfully on just about every step of the journey. We had a long and almost disastrous love affair with bigness, technology, success, and modernity.

Now we understand some of the consequences—anonymity, loss of identity, dehumanization, suppression of individuality, a sense of powerlessness, barriers to significant human communication, and the introduction into human relations of greater abstractness and artificiality than most people can tolerate.

The reaction of the citizen has been more profound and pervasive than anyone could have predicted. It goes far beyond assaults on the establishment by noisy dissidents, far beyond the alienation of the young. There is in all segments of society an undercurrent of hostility toward institutional life, toward impersonal efficiency, toward organization, toward the endless small indignities of an administered age. We are tired of being manipulated by the unseen controllers of our lives.

The essential requirement is that large-scale organization, technology, and the success ethic not be allowed to triumph over human values, nor over individual meaning and relevance, nor over those longed-for and elusive ideals of love, brotherhood, and cooperation.

A more subtle and difficult requirement is that the interlocking mechanisms of the society not fragment the individual. There is a longing for wholeness, for authenticity, for immediate experience, for the emotional, symbolic, nonrational elements of life that do not automatically flow from the functional efficiency of large-scale organizations. There is a feeling that fantasy, drama, and the life of the senses have been squeezed out of our intricately organized society.

So far, the widespread hostility to institutions has not resulted in any significant change, chiefly because the hostility has been so diffuse, so fiercely aimless, that it hasn't hit any significant targets. Flailing indignation isn't enough. Anger has too often expressed itself in the unrealistic hope that technology and large-scale organization would just go away. But they won't. We cannot live without them.

The much harder but achievable goal is to make technology serve human values, to redesign large-scale organization in such a way as to serve individual human needs. But those tasks cannot be accomplished by individuals so far gone in scorn for their society that constructive action appears hopeless. When we begin to restore the gravely damaged relation between the individual and society, then we will begin to see that far from scorning his society, the individual must nurture it. He must work to make it more effective as an instrument of freedom, an instrument at the disposal of the individual. He must make it the shield of his liberties, the guarantor of his dignity, the seedbed of his future.

That is a lot to ask. For three generations of skeptics

and rebels, stretching back at least to World War I in this country and back to the nineteenth-century bohemians in France, the appropriate and fashionable attitudes toward one's own society have been hostility, anger, irritation, resentment, contempt, and a sense of separateness. To ask them now to nurture their society may push them beyond the limits of tolerance.

Yet some of us must do it. We must criticize our country, but care about it. We must see its weaknesses, but build its strength. We must see the hypocrisy of outworn visions, but not be afraid to lend ourselves to new visions.

As the citizen begins to see the logic of nurturing his society, he will see other things more clearly. He will see that in our rebellion against the sterility of large-scale organization, we have been moving fairly swiftly toward an equally sterile disorganization. He will see that chaos, aimlessness, and anomie are not really viable alternatives.

He will see that chaos must be replaced by form and pattern—but form and pattern that enrich rather than drain life of meaning; that aimlessness must be replaced by humanly relevant purpose; that anomie must be replaced by life-enriching principle.

PROBLEMS TO SOLVE

Very few of the problems facing this nation are simple. Some are so complex and puzzling that it will take us years to solve them. Our present understanding of how to resolve the problems of war and peace, of our economy, of urban chaos, of adequate health care, of early childhood education is limited at best.

We shall have to address ourselves to those problems

with patience and even humility, a willingness to experiment, a determination to learn by past failures, and above all an intention to keep at it. What we must avoid is an enthusiastic burst of hastily conceived social programs, followed by disappointment with those programs, and then later another cycle of enthusiasm—disappointment, always with too much hurry and optimism on the upswing, too much petulant rejection on the downswing. We cannot tackle the nation's problems like moody children. We must stay at it, experiment, learn, measure results, and try again.

LEADERSHIP

The emphasis I have put on citizen action and initiative is not intended to diminish in any way the importance of leadership. An alive, aware citizenry will not lessen the need for leaders; it will ensure better leadership. People get the leaders they deserve.

Effective leadership is essential to cope with the inertia present in any social system. Systemic inertia is characteristic of all societies, but especially true of this nation. Our system of checks and balances dilutes the thrust of positive action. The multiplicity of interests inherent in our pluralism acts as a powerful brake on significant public initiatives. The system is designed to grind to a halt between crises. James Madison constructed it in such a way that it simply will not move without vigorous, driving leadership. I've often wondered why he didn't say so. Having in mind his brilliant contemporaries, I suppose it just never occurred to him that the day might come when leadership would be lacking.

It's more than a question of leadership at the top.

We'd all be better off if we stopped looking for a savior. We need leadership at every level and in every segment of society—not only in government but in business, the professions, labor, the universities, the minority communities. We need leadership that will move vigorously to keep each of those special worlds abreast of the swift social changes that are wracking the nation and the world. But even more, we need leadership that has some understanding of how all the special worlds fit together into a functioning society.

We now have about as wrong-headed an attitude toward leadership as a society could have. We tolerate mediocrity in our leaders and then exhibit contempt for them. We should do precisely the reverse: demand excellence of our leaders and then respect them. It would be pleasant to believe that we are blameless in this—that we want desperately to respect our leaders but cannot. But there is in us, alas, a streak of low envy that makes contempt for leaders a pleasurable emotion—for some of us, all of the time, and for all of us, some of the time.

We must demand of our leaders that they speak to the best in us. It is too easy for leaders to appeal to prejudice, fear, anger, and selfishness, and to find villains to blame for our troubles. There is in us something better than fear, anger, prejudice, and selfishness, something better than the comfortable inclination to blame others—and our leaders must call it forth.

But no matter how enlightened our leaders, they cannot do the job alone. Neither the President nor any other elected official, caught as they are in the constraints of political life, can accomplish what needs to be done. They can *help*—and *be helped*—to accomplish it if something else is happening, something much deeper than the political emotions of election day. They can be helped if the American people begin to recognize their own shaping role in renovating the instruments of self-government.

The American people are capable of that—but first they must experience a few concrete victories in tackling their problems and actually solving them.

When this nation began in the 1770s, it had a population of about 3 million, yet it produced at least a dozen statesmen of extraordinary quality—individuals with an exceptional gift for leadership, with intellectual gifts, and a capacity for action, capable of the highest order of statecraft. Today, with sixty times greater population, we surely have far more men and women of that caliber in our population. But where are they? For the most part, they simply do not enter public life. And those who do find themselves trapped in institutions that cannot be made to function effectively.

We must bring about a renaissance in politics. We must make it possible for our ablest, most gifted individuals to be active in that part of our national life. Men and women of the greatest integrity, character, and courage should turn to public life as a natural duty and a natural outlet for their talents.

Does that seem inordinately ambitious? It is. This is no time for small plans.

IN COMMON CAUSE

Our nation is in the gravest possible danger —danger of losing its vitality and confidence and coherence as a society. Citizen action can play a significant role in averting that danger.

Government of, by, and for the people is the most exhilarating venture man has ever undertaken. Also the most difficult. It puts a giant responsibility on citizens and we have not lived up to it.

The citizen can bring our political and governmental institutions back to life, make them responsive and accountable, and keep them honest. No one else can. The one condition for the rebirth of this nation is a rebirth of individual responsibility.

If a citizens' movement can prove its capacity to achieve specific and important objectives, the citizen may recover the hope—now virtually lost—that he can regain command of the vast and invisible bureaucratic processes that dominate his life. He may rediscover that the vitality of his society is inseparable from his own creative part in it. He may even learn how much we need each other.

APPENDIX A

The First Year of Common Cause

IN THE SUMMER of 1970, Common Cause was created as a nationwide membership organization to speak out in the public interest and in behalf of the individual American. The initial conception was reflected in the first announcement:

> Common Cause is a national citizens' lobby. We will lobby in the public interest at all levels of government, but especially at the federal level. We will assist our members to speak and act in behalf of legislation designed to solve the nation's problems. We will press for a reordering of national priorities. We will also press for the revitalization of the public process, to make our political and governmental institutions more responsive to the needs of the nation and the will of its citizens.
>
> We will uphold the public interest against all comers —special interests, self-seeking politicians, self-perpetuating bureaucrats, industry, professional groups.
>
> Fortunately, there are many, many Americans who would like to help rebuild this nation. But they don't know where or how to begin. They recognize that national priorities must be revised, but they don't know how to go about it. They are shocked by the facts of poverty and pollution and racial conflict, but they don't know what to do.

Common Cause will help those citizens discover what they can do as individuals.

Before the announcement was made, as word of the project circulated in Washington, the idea evoked profound skepticism. Worldly-wise observers of the political scene assured us that there were already too many organizations, that we were too idealistic, that there was no precedent for what we were doing, that citizens' movements always fail. They assured us that the effort would never get off the ground because we would not be able to command national attention nor—in a time of national apathy—get members.

We knew that their skepticism wasn't groundless. We were not naïve. We knew it was possible that our call to action would evoke little interest; and if that happened we knew that there would be no way to retrieve the failure.

Fortunately, the knowing observers were wrong. No sooner did the word get out of our intention to form the organization, than mail began to pour in. Long before our plans were sufficiently complete to make an official announcement, stories appeared in newspapers all over the country telling of our plan. And the volume of letters increased.

We hadn't yet decided on a name. We didn't know what the dues would be. But the letters came, rising to some 200 a day before we made our official announcement and launched our membership drive.

THE INITIAL RESPONSE

After the announcement was officially made, the mail built up to 1,000 letters a day. The response to our test mailing was four times as great as the direct mail experts had predicted. It came from all fifty states, from small towns and suburban communities as well as big cities, from teen-agers and retired people, from blue-collar workers and minority people, from business executives and students.

We set a membership goal of 100,000 for the first year. To our astonishment, we achieved it in twenty-three weeks. By the time we reached our first anniversary we had 200,000 members.

ACHIEVEMENTS

The rapid build-up of membership was exhilarating but inconclusive. It proved that a lot of people were ready for something that was described to them as a citizens' lobby. The question remained as to whether the organization would fulfill their hopes.

The possibility that we would lose more battles than we won didn't worry us. We knew that if we thought too much about the box score we might be tempted to choose the easy fights. We decided to take on the difficult ones and do the best possible. It was clear to us that it was going to take a lot of battles, well fought, to give this country back to its people.

It is presumptuous for any organization to claim credit for a legislative victory. First credit goes to the legislators who voted the right way; and, beyond that, credit must be shared with many dedicated citizens' groups working toward similar goals. With those qualifications, here are some of the battles in which we have been engaged.

We lobbied in support of S. 3867, The Employment and Training Opportunities Act in the Senate in the fall of 1970. The bill passed, and Senator Gaylord

Nelson said, "Common Cause played an absolutely crucial role."

In January 1971, we were credited by members of Congress and journalists with helping to produce the first dent in the antiquated seniority system—but it wasn't a big enough dent to be called a major victory. We also sought the ouster of three of the most tyrannical committee chairmen in the House and failed in the attempt.

We joined with many other citizens' groups in successfully opposing the SST.

We fought for a series of measures designed to bring an end to the Vietnam war by a specified date. We helped, for example, to bring the House to its first recorded vote on the war. It says something about the functioning of Congress that the war divided the nation in bitterness and violence for six long years before the House of Representatives got around to voting on it. In tackling issues of this sort, we learned that we could take on the toughest of legislative efforts and hold our own. We carried the end-the-war effort to the people with full page ads in the 150 newspapers around the country and with a television show that was seen throughout the nation.

In late 1970, we helped get a campaign-financing reform bill through both the Senate and House but the President vetoed it. Then in the next session of Congress, we helped in passage of a bill with media spending limits and useful disclosure features, which the President signed. We also filed suit against the major parties, seeking to restrain them from violating the campaign-spending laws. Although the law suit became moot as a result of the new legislation, Herbert Alexander, the leading scholarly authority on campaign financing, said that the court action by Common Cause "undoubtedly helped prod the Congress into action."

Common Cause was the chief citizen organization lobbying for the constitutional amendment giving the vote to eighteen-year-olds. The amendment passed the Senate unanimously on March 9 (96–0) and the House overwhelmingly (400–19) on March 23. We then worked for ratification in every state where there was a reasonable possibility of its being considered—and it was ratified by the necessary thirty-eight states more swiftly than any earlier amendment.

Common Cause also undertook a nationwide campaign to eliminate barriers to voter registration and to open up the process of delegate selection in both major parties.

Long before we had completed our first year, journalists and politicians were freely admitting that we were a "force." Writing in the *Christian Science Monitor* on May 23, 1971, Godfrey Sperling said, "At this point all that can be said is that Common Cause in less than a year has made a significant impact on the government and on those who run the government."

NONPARTISANSHIP

Common Cause is nonpartisan. But it is deeply involved in politics—citizen politics in the public interest, but politics nonetheless. It must have on its board and staff at least some people who are thoroughly versed in politics—Republican, Democrat, and Independent— which means that they will have been part of political campaigns in the past.

If we are to be effective we must often do things that evoke resistance and anger from people involved in the political machinery. Sometimes they will accuse us of partisanship. Occasionally, they may even believe it.

We can expect the criticism to continue. Some of it will be justified, since we will surely make mistakes. But some of the criticism will be the inevitable consequence of hard-fought battles. Getting our institutions back into working order is going to be painful and some people aren't going to like it. If no one complains, we probably aren't doing the job.

Many of the battles we engage in inevitably have partisan overtones. When we first lobbied to control campaign spending, the Republican party appeared to be the target of our attack, since it seemed at that time to be less enthusiastic about controls than the Democrats. But at the same moment we were attacking the seniority system, with Democrats as the chief targets (since Democrats hold the chairmanships). In neither case was our purpose partisan.

We work in close collaboration with both Republican and Democratic senators, congressmen, governors, and state legislators week in and week out.

GOVERNING

In the course of our first year we set up a system through which the membership elects members to the board, and we held our first election. At this writing the second annual election of board members is about to take place.

The Governing Board will ultimately number eighty. Sixty will be elected by the members, and the remaining twenty will be appointed by the Board itself with a view to correcting any imbalances in representation of women, minority groups, or geographical areas. The membership of the Governing Board as it now stands is listed in Appendix B.

Of course, in any voluntary citizens' organization like

Common Cause, the most conclusive vote cast by the individual is his decision to join or resign. His joining is in effect a vote for the movement; his resignation or failure to renew membership is a vote against. Thus, collectively, the members hold life-or-death control over the organization. If enough of them fail to renew their memberships, that will be the end of Common Cause.

THE CHOOSING OF ISSUES

When Common Cause was founded in September of 1970, there was published in the first newsletter a list of fifteen proposed agenda items. We then carried out a mail referendum, asking members to rate the proposed agenda items according to the priority they wished them to be given. Six months later we repeated the process. The results of the two ratings were very similar, so we know with some certainty what the priorities of our members are. (See Appendix C.) So far we have operated entirely within the top seven priorities as indicated by the members.

In addition to such systematically gathered information, we have abundant nonstatistical evidence of our members' views on issues. We receive a vast amount of correspondence from members, a substantial portion of which is devoted to discussion of issues. And the top staff meets with members all over the country. Large membership meetings (with 500 to 3,000 in attendance) take place in one or another part of the country almost every week. With few exceptions, the meeting halls are set up with microphones in the aisle and ample time is provided for questions and answers. In one after another city, long hours are spent in dialogue with small groups of members. Board members, staff members, and members of the general public also contribute ideas as to issues Common Cause should tackle.

All of the suggestions for new issues are placed before the New Issues Committee of the Governing Board, which decides which matters are worthy of further study and exploration.

The staff of Common Cause, working within the framework of members' top priorities and the decisions of the New Issues Committee, undertakes intensive study of possible courses of action, and develops tentative plans for legislation or litigation to achieve specific objectives.

Finally, recommendations are placed before the Governing Board, which debates the issues and makes the final decisions. Members of the Governing Board are elected by the membership. The fact that Common Cause does not take on any issue that it does not intend to fight to the finish means that it can tackle only a few fights at a time and must choose new issues with care.

If clearance is given by the Board, the necessary next steps are taken:

a) dissemination of information among members to give them the information to act.
b) lobbying in one or both houses of Congress by the staff and by members.
c) establishment of alliances with other citizens' groups working toward the same objective.
d) an information campaign to bring the issue to public attention.

WHAT MEMBERS DO

We do not expect every member to be active. Some cannot give personal time to the organization, and take the view that in paying their dues they are supporting those who *can* give time. But there are other individuals who want very much to be personally active—and there is virtually no limit to how effective these individuals can be. A good many people imagine that the task of the citizen in a "citizens' lobby" is simply to write his congressman occasionally, but the possibilities are infinitely varied.

Members write to their local newspapers. They urge their church, unions, or lodges to discuss Common Cause issues. Some of them take the trouble to get to know the news director of their local TV station and the editor of their local paper. Some have used listener participation programs on TV or radio to bring the issues to public attention. Some inform themselves as to the local groups or individuals who have made major contributions to the campaigns of their senators and congressman. Some have bought advertisements in their local newspapers in behalf of Common Cause.

Another extremely important form of local action is the setting up of telephone campaigns within congressional districts. A small group of Common Cause members, working closely with the national office, recruits and trains a volunteer telephone team that sets out to reach the maximum number of Common Cause members (and nonmembers) in that district. The purpose is to alert members that one of the Common Cause issues has reached a crucial point in the legislative process—a point at which members should communicate their views to their elected representatives. The technique has proven remarkably effective. The congressman soon becomes acutely aware of the Common Cause position.

We provide the kinds of information that make it possible for our members to act effectively. We help them find the points of leverage. We keep them up-to-date on important issues before the Congress and let them know what they might do at any given time to influence those issues.

Some individuals who are actively concerned with the issues of the day seek newer and more exhilarating modes of citizen action. We understand that impulse. But first things first. As Vince Lombardi said, "First learn to block and tackle." A citizen must understand the processes of self-government. He must learn to use intelligently the instruments that are available to him. His capacity to make his views felt at the federal level is particularly crucial. The public interest can be benefitted or butchered by the day-to-day decisions of federal agencies or actions of Congress.

Implicit in all of this is the idea that members will do the kind of homework that will make them effective in citizen action. They should learn all they can about their congressman. They ought to know what his stated positions are, what actions he has taken, what his strengths and weaknesses are. They should have the same knowledge of their two senators, their governor, and their state assemblyman. We help them do their homework.

The participation by members is crucial. A key objective of Common Cause is to give the citizen heightened participation in his government, and to give him the moral reinforcement of knowing his own efforts are matched and strengthened by the efforts of hundreds of thousands of fellow citizens.

MULTIPLE ISSUES

When we launched Common Cause, even our friends warned us of what might be called the "multi-issue dilemma." Most citizens' movements, they reminded us, have rallied around a single issue—the war, the environment, family planning, and the like. The participants in such a movement may disagree on many other issues, but they are held together by an overpowering concern to solve *that specific problem.*

In forming Common Cause we faced the obvious question: what could possibly hold together the members of an organization that tackled a dozen different problems. Wouldn't a member be likely to agree heartily on how we handled one question but strongly resent the way we handled another issue?

The first thing to be said, after eighteen months experience, is that the organization has held together somehow. And surveys indicate that the members are on the whole quite satisfied, even though they may disagree with one or more of the positions we have taken. A lawyer in St. Louis probably spoke for most members when he said to me, "I think the average member will allow you about 15 percent 'errors'—that is, positions he doesn't personally agree with. Beyond that, look out!"

There are several factors that might account for the tendency of the membership not to split over the multiple issues we take on.

1. The recruitment literature, whether direct mail or advertisement, reveals fairly clearly the over-all philosophy of the organization, so that presumably those who join are people disposed to agree with that philosophy.

2. We have taken pains to find out what problems our members want us to tackle and have worked on those.

3. Throughout almost all of the various issues we have tackled, there runs the binding theme of making our instruments of self-government more responsive and accountable and providing greater access to them on the part of citizens; and that is a theme on which we all can agree.

FINANCING

Common Cause is incorporated under the laws of the District of Columbia as a nonprofit organization. It has been granted permission to carry on its activities in all states requiring registration. It has also been granted tax-exempt status by the Internal Revenue Service, but contributions are not tax deductible because our avowed purpose is to influence legislation.

The funds required to inaugurate the membership campaign were provided by a substantial number of contributors who believed that an effective citizens' lobby was needed to make our government responsible and accountable. At this writing, the budget is based entirely on the receipt of membership dues. The organization still receives a good many contributions—most of them in the $5–$10 range—but dues provide the economic base on which the organization operates.

An independent audit is made by Price Waterhouse of all funds received and spent, and an audited financial statement is available on request.

Governing Board of Common Cause

ARENT, Albert E.
Arent, Fox, Kintner, Plotkin
and Kahn
Washington, D. C.

*ARONSON, Arnold
Secretary, Leadership Confer-
ence on Civil Rights
New York, New York

*BARONI, Monsignor Geno
Director, Center for Urban
Ethnic Affairs
Washington, D. C.

BECK, Lowell
Associate Executive Director
American Bar Association
Chicago, Illinois

*BENSON, Mrs. Bruce B.
President, League of Women
Voters of the United States
Washington, D. C.

*BLUMENTHAL, Richard
Yale Law School Student
New Haven, Connecticut

CHEEK, Dr. James E.
President, Howard University

Washington, D. C.

CINTRON, Humberto
Chairman, Concerned Citizens
of East Harlem, Inc.
New York, New York

COHEN, Wilbur J.
Dean, School of Education
University of Michigan
Ann Arbor, Michigan

CONWAY, Jack T.
President, Common Cause
Washington, D. C.

DYSON, Charles
Chairman of the Board
The Dyson-Kissner Corpora-
tion
New York, New York

EHRLICH, Dr. Paul R.
Professor of Biology
Stanford University
Stanford, California

FULLER, Margaret
Vice Chairman
Independent Voters of Ohio
Cincinnati, Ohio

* Denotes member of Executive Committee April 20, 1972.

125

FURNESS, Betty
Consumer Protection
Consultant
Hartsdale, New York

*GARDNER, John W.
Chairman, Common Cause
Washington, D. C.

HARRIS, Mrs. Fred R.
President, Americans for
Indian Opportunity
Washington, D. C.

HEIGHT, Dorothy I.
President, National Council of
Negro Women, Inc.
Washington, D. C.

*HEISKELL, Andrew
Chairman of the Board
TIME, Inc.
New York, New York

*HERNANDEZ,
Mrs. Aileen C.
Western Representative
National Committee Against
Discrimination in Housing
San Francisco, California

*HERTER, Mrs. Christian A.,
Jr.
Washington, D. C.

JACKSON, Reverend Jesse
National Director
People United to Save
Humanity
Chicago, Illinois

KEENAN, Joseph D.
International Secretary
International Brotherhood of
Electrical Workers
Washington, D. C.

*KILBERG, Barbara Green
Attorney, Arnold and Porter
Washington, D. C.

KOLDYKE, Martin
Frontenac Company
Chicago, Illinois

LINDSAY, Margot Coffin
Co-Chairman
WBZ Call for Action
Lincoln, Massachusetts

*MARTIN, Ruby Grant
Fellow, Washington Research
Project
Washington, D. C.

MYERSON, Martin
President, University of
Pennsylvania
Philadelphia, Pennsylvania

MILLER, Herbert S.
Deputy Director, Institute of
Criminal Law & Procedure
Georgetown University Law
Center
Washington, D. C.

*OLIVAREZ, Ms. Graciela
Director, Institute for Social
Research and Development
University of New Mexico
Albuquerque, New Mexico

PARIS, Susan V.
Founder, Vermont Project for
Public Interest Law
Bennington, Vermont

SAMUEL, Howard D.
Vice President
Amalgamated Clothing
Workers of America
New York, New York

APPENDIX C

Members' Ratings of Issues

THE ITEMS on which the members were asked to express a preference, first in October 1970 and again in June 1971, were as follows (the items are listed according to the priority that the members assigned to them in the latter of the two referendums):

1. Withdrawal of all American forces from Vietnam on an orderly and scheduled timetable; an intensified effort to negotiate with the Soviet Union an end to the nuclear arms race; a marked reduction in defense spending; continued responsible U.S. involvement in the world.

2. Immediate and far-reaching moves to conserve, protect, and enhance the environment, including realistically strong sanctions where appropriate against those who pollute it.

3. Overhaul and revitalization of government at national, state, and local levels to create effective and responsive institutions and processes.

4. Equal opportunity in every aspect of American life, particularly in education, housing, employment,

and voting. Effective action at every level against discrimination based on race, ethnic background, or sex.

5. Overhaul of the criminal justice system to achieve more effective ways of dealing with lawlessness, whether street crime, organized crime, corporate crime, or official corruption—with emphasis on modernization of the courts, redirection of penal and correctional institutions, and improved police training and practices in both law enforcement and community relations.

6. The elimination of poverty through sound management of the economy, through adequate income-maintenance programs coupled with training and employment opportunities; through improved social security; through early childhood education and similar measures to get at the roots of poverty.

7. Overhaul of our wholly inadequate system for the delivery of health care so that it serves all citizens equitably, efficiently, and with regard for their dignity.

8. Improved education at every level, with emphasis on correcting present inequities in resource distribution between rural and urban, urban and suburban areas, and among different regions, and vigorous encouragement of breakthroughs in educational methods.

9. Public and private sector action to fulfill within a decade the national commitment made twenty-one years ago of decent housing in a suitable living environment for every American family.

10. Improved and intensified programs to foster family planning, here and around the world.

11. Improved urban transportation through greatly increased federal investments and innovations, and strengthened metropolitan regional agencies empowered to plan and act for all modes of urban transportation.

12. A carefully planned program to accommodate the substantial population growth expected between now and the year 2000, so that the necessary creation of new cities, rehabilitation of existing cities, and programs of rural economic development will conserve not only natural resources but human values.

13. An employment program to assure every American the skill training to enter the job market or to rise in it, and to assure him a job when he is trained.

14. Consumer protection through measures to insure corporate accountability in regard to all goods and services; rigorously applied penalties for exploitation and fraud; and strengthening of consumer agencies at federal, state, and local levels.

15. Sustained economic growth to provide employment opportunities for a growing population, and price stability to protect earnings, savings, and fixed incomes. Tax and fiscal policies that promote the broad public interest rather than special interests.